W9-BYU-370

TWAYNE'S WORLD AUTHORS SERIES

A Survey of the World's Literature

Sylvia E. Bowman, Indiana University

GENERAL EDITOR

NEW ZEALAND

Joseph Jones, University of Texas

EDITOR

Frank Sargeson

(TWAS 75)

TWAYNE'S WORLD AUTHORS SERIES (TWAS)

The purpose of TWAS is to survey the major writers —novelists, dramatists, historians, poets, philosophers, and critics—of the nations of the world. Among the national literatures covered are those of Australia, Canada, China, Eastern Europe, France, Germany, Greece, India, Italy, Japan, Latin America, New Zealand, Poland, Russia, Scandinavia, Spain, and the African nations, as well as Hebrew, Yiddish, and Latin Classical literatures. This survey is complemented by Twayne's United States Authors Series and English Authors Series

The intent of each volume in these series is to present a critical-analytical study of the works of the writer; to include biographical and historical material that may be necessary for understanding, appreciation, and critical appraisal of the writer; and to present all material in clear, concise English—but not to vitiate the scholarly content of the work by doing so.

Frank Sargeson

By H. WINSTON RHODES

University of Canterbury

Twayne Publishers, Inc. :: New York

Preface

"YOUR work has had, in the past twenty years, a liberating
influence on the literature of this country. . . . It is not
often that a writer can be said to have become a symbol in his
own time." These two sentences are part of a letter signed by
sixteen well-known authors of short stories and novels on the
occasion of Frank Sargeson's fiftieth birthday in 1953. They appeared in the pages of the New Zealand Quarterly, *Landfall.*

Sargeson had published his early sketches in *Tomorrow*, a
journal of the thirties; he had contributed to *Landfall* in 1950-51
fragments of a still unpublished autobiography, *Up onto the
Roof and Down Again;* but, at the time of this tribute he had
produced only a very small number of volumes, including *A
Man and his Wife, That Summer and Other Stories*, and *I Saw
in My Dream.* Portions of these, or the complete books, had
been published not only in New Zealand but also in England
and America, and *That Summer* had been translated into French
and published in Paris; but Sargeson had certainly not been a
prolific writer. His name was not widely recognized even in the
country of his birth. Yet, in the opinion of fellow writers, as
well as of critics of some standing, his achievements had justified
the description of him as "a liberating influence" and as one
who had become "a symbol in his own time."

"It is scarcely possible," wrote Walter Allen from England,
"to imagine any task more difficult than that of a pioneer of a
new literature. By definition he has no tradition to help him. . . .
I am impressed by the amount Sargeson must have had to

unlearn before he could write the stories of *A Man and his Wife*. He has, in other words, to make his own tradition." [1] D'Arcy Cresswell, the author of *A Poet's Progress*, recorded that when "Sargeson's *Conversation with my Uncle* first appeared in the mid-thirties it was as though the first wasp had arrived, a bright, aggressive little thing with a new and menacing buzz." [2]

Such remarks might seem to imply that New Zealand literature began only after the economic depression of the thirties with Frank Sargeson; but even during what may be called the 'post-pioneer period,' which lasted roughly to that time when as a young girl in Wellington Katherine Mansfield was writing in her diary, "Go anywhere. Don't stay here," there had been the early narratives of European New Zealanders, the unfortunately sterile productions of men and women who still regarded themselves as exiles, who observed through English eyes, and in their writing made the vain attempt to adapt what were usually inferior models to a strange and alien situation. They were caught inextricably between two worlds. They succeeded in writing only disguised guidebooks to the unfamiliar or floundered among problems and themes for which they possessed neither chart nor compass to help them in their exploratory attempts. They had neither a style suited to their purpose nor become identified with the new environment in which they found themselves. Their books are interesting only to the New Zealand literary historian or to those who wish to return to the not always clumsy records of earlier activities and attitudes.

There were novels such as *Philosopher Dick* (1891), by George Chamier, or *The Heart of the Bush* (1910), by Edith Searle Grossman, which attempted to deal with themes not unfamiliar to writers of a later generation, themes of adjustment and the failure of adjustment, of race relations, of the contrast between an older European culture and the new pioneering world, of the hostility of a philistine but hard-working community to the subtleties of thought and emotion and the conventions of gracious living. Even the titles of many of these earlier productions carry with them the suggestion of pioneer attempts to record the past before it has been fully understood or assimilated into a vigorous and developing tradition. *The Land of the Lost* and *The Call of the Bush*, both by William Satchell, the author of the later historical reconstruction *The Greenstone Door* (1913), were written soon after the turn of the century; and there were such collections of short stories as *Tales of a Dying Race* (1901), *Where the White Man Treads* (1905), and Blanche Baughan's *Brown Bread from a Colonial Oven* (1912). Jane Mander's recently republished novel, *The Story of a New Zealand River* (1920), is certainly the best known and probably the most successful of the attempts to give fictional form to the conflict between two worlds and between two generations; and in *Something Childish*, published posthumously in 1924, Katherine Mansfield, who had fled from the New Zealand scene, returned to the memories of her childhood to produce a handful of stories which are among the best in her collected works.

There was little in these pioneering attempts, little even in Katherine Mansfield's sensitive evocations of the New Zealand that was "in her very bones" that could help a dedicated young writer in his search for answers to questions that worried him. Much later, in a broadcast, "Writing a Novel," he was to recall his disappointment with his own early attempts, and how only then he began to read every New Zealand novel he could find; but, he continued, "it seemed that in almost every case language which did not differ very greatly from that used by English novelists was used to deal with the material of New Zealand life." [3] It was not only the language, however, but the material of New Zealand life itself that had not been explored sufficiently to provide anything in the nature of a tradition from which young writers could draw nourishment or from which they could diverge. Frank Sargeson was forced to begin at the beginning.

A definitive study of a writer who still may have much to offer is not possible, but in the pages that follow the attempt will be made to explore the path which Sargeson followed, the obstacles he had to overcome, and the "liberating" achievement of a writer who, in the opinion of many, has already become "a symbol in his own time" to the literature of New Zealand.

My thanks are due to the following publishers for permission to quote from Frank Sargeson's works: Blackwood & Janet Paul; the Caxton Press; MacGibbon & Kee; also to Charles Brasch for material published in *Landfall*, to Bill Pearson and Blackwood & Janet Paul for allowing access to the Bibliography of Frank Sargeson's work before it appeared in the *Collected Stories*, to the New Zealand Broadcasting Corporation and Doris Gaudin for assistance in making a typescript of "Writing a Novel," to Helen Shaw for quotations from *The Puritan and the Waif*, and to Vera Ross for typing. I am greatly endebted to Frank Sargeson for his helpful cooperation, but must stress that he is not responsible for the use I have made of his manuscripts, nor for my interpretation of biographical information.

H. W. R.

University of Canterbury, Christchurch.

Contents

Chronology

1903   March 23: Frank Sargeson born at Hamilton, New Zealand.

1917   Attending Hamilton High School.

1920   Begins sitting Auckland University College extramural examinations in law.

1925   Working in a Hamilton law office. Leaves home and Hamilton.

1926   Lives in a bach (small, cabin-type house) owned by his father at Takapuna, Auckland. Admitted as solicitor and works in an Auckland law office.

1927   Leaves for England.

1928   Returns to New Zealand and finds work in a Wellington government department.

1929   A breakdown; goes to live with his uncle at Okahakura, where he writes a novel (unpublished).

1931   Moves to Auckland and lives in the Takapuna bach, which has remained his permanent headquarters. Registers as unemployed and during the depression works at various manual jobs.

1931–35   Writes many stories and free-lance articles, but very little published.

1935   Begins writing for *Tomorrow*. Labour Government raises single man's sustenance to £1 a week.

1935–40 More than forty short stories and sketches published in *Tomorrow* and other journals.

1936 *Conversation with My Uncle and Other Sketches.*

1939–45 Surgical tuberculosis prevents the possibility of war service. Obtains Invalidity Benefit.

1940 *A Man and His Wife.* Story, "The Making of a New Zealander," awarded first prize (equal) in the Centennial Literary Competitions.

1940–46 Growing reputation. Stories published in *Penguin New Writing, Folios of New Writing, Bulletin, The Listener* (London), *Angry Penguins* (Adelaide), *New Writing, Daylight,* etc.

1945 *When the Wind Blows.*

1946 *That Summer and Other Stories.*

1947 Granted a small literary pension of £3 a week to replace Invalidity Benefit. Sargeson's father transfers Takapuna bach to his son.

1948 House-study built on Takapuna section: Sargeson's uncle helps with the house just before his death in this year. Sargeson had paid frequent visits to his uncle's farm at Okahakura since he had come to live at Takapuna.

1949 *I Saw in My Dream.*

1952 Receives the Hubert Church prize for "Up onto the Roof and Down Again," published in *Landfall.*

1953 Letter published in *Landfall,* signed by sixteen prominent New Zealand writers in honour of Sargeson's fiftieth birthday.

1956 *I for One.*

1961 "A Time for Sowing" performed in Auckland.

1962 "The Cradle and the Egg" performed in Auckland.

1964 *Collected Stories. Wrestling with the Angel.*

1965 Alison Duff's bronze bust of Frank Sargeson (commissioned by the Arts Advisory Council) presented to the Auckland Public Library. Receives Katherine Mansfield Award for the short story, "Just Trespassing, Thanks." *Memoirs of a Peon.*

1967 *The Hangover.*

CHAPTER 1

The Making of a New Zealander

"Puritanism is an awful disease."

JANE MANDER

I *Waiamihea*

THE biography of a writer may, and very often does, become an end in itself, a substitute for receptivity, an evasion of any serious attempt to examine and explore the conscious intention of his imaginative creations. It is easy to fall into what has been called the personal heresy, to mistake irrelevant and impertinent details for critical illumination, or to imagine that a simple equation can be made between the man who suffers and enjoys and the artist who creates.

Referring to a correspondent in *Tomorrow* who had commented on his early stories, Frank Sargeson wrote: "[He] is wrong if he assumes that the incidents and characters . . . are taken directly from life, or that the 'I' necessarily represents myself. For an understanding of the spirit behind the sketches I would suggest a re-reading of Whitman, or Sherwood Anderson." [1] Nevertheless, it has been suggested more than once, for example by E. P. Dawson in her discussion[2] of *I Saw in My Dream*, that Sargeson's writings are largely autobiographical. This is an over-simplification, for the relation of a writer to his work is generally more varied and more complex than most people are prepared to admit. One of the reasons why Sargeson's autobiography, *Up onto the Roof and Down Again*, has not been published in its extended version is that the author realized that parts of it could be used in other ways. "Used," however, is in this context a deceptive word, for the writer's imagination becomes a crucible in which the personal is *dissolved* and so

13

changes that what emerges bears little relation to the raw material, the private and particular truth, that began the process, "life being," said Henry James, "all inclusion and confusion. and art being all discrimination and selection."

The story of Frank Sargeson's early life deserves attention—not because it is essential to an understanding and appreciation of his writings, but because in a very special way it vividly portrays the growth and development of a New Zealand writer and therefore reveals many of the problems associated with creative writing in a young country. *I Saw in My Dream* contains a description of the Maori house where Rangi lived. It "had a garden that was untidy with weeds yet bright with red geraniums; and on the gate you could make out the word: WAIAMIHEA. But it must have been painted there a long time ago—you could hardly read the letters now." [3] Much later in the book Johnny remarks: "I used to think Waiamihea was a proper Maori name. But it's not. Cedric told me. It means Why-am-I-here. See?" [4] Waiamihea may be described as the theme song of writers in a young country. When Sargeson was in England in 1927 he was greatly impressed by Joyce's *A Portrait of the Artist as a Young Man*, so impressed that he began to write thousands of words of his own "Portrait," only to discover, when he turned to read what he had written, that it was "incurably unreadable." [5] There was nothing surprising in this failure. He was not yet sufficiently detached from the self he was beginning to discover. He could not yet recognize the very different selves of the family and social life from which he had become separated. He had not yet learnt to establish a spiritual home in or outside his boyhood environment. He was still asking the question "Why-am-I-here?" and the dedication and full commitment of the artist was not yet complete. Since Katherine Mansfield fled to England from the small-town environment of Wellington, many New Zealand writers have followed in her footsteps and fully demonstrated the significance of WAIAMIHEA. Sargeson returned to New Zealand after a year abroad, returned to stay, but not in the Hamilton of his boyhood.

In the 1870's Hamilton was a small settlement of fewer than 700 people, divided by the Waikato river and situated eighty-six miles south of Auckland. It had been founded in 1864 by military settlers of the 4th Waikato Regiment who, encouraged by the New Zealand government and by the munificent offer of free land which belonged to the Maoris, had established a frontier post on the site of a former Maori village. Many of these over-sanguine settlers experienced hard times, for, although the disgraceful Waikato invasion had dispossessed the Maoris who had retreated further east or south to the King country, the government was not quick to respond to the real grievances voiced by its frontiersmen; but by the 1870's new settlers were arriving and schemes for public works had begun to make the small township a more habitable place.

Among these later settlers were Frank Sargeson's paternal grandparents. They arrived in Auckland by sailing ship, travelled by train as far as Mercer, and then by paddle-steamer up the Waikato to Hamilton. They were both Londoners from the east end, although there was a Welsh strain on the grandfather's side and the "wonderful grandmother," with her dark colouring and black eyes, reminded her grandson (he knew her only during the last years in Auckland) of the gypsies he had encountered in storybooks. *A Personal Memory*, which he wrote for the Auckland literary periodical, *Mate*, in 1957 recalls with evident affection her large soft face which when she was going to laugh "would begin to wrinkle and twitch, soon her whole soft body would begin to wobble, her great soft chin would jerk up and down, and her wrinkled-up eyes would begin to stream." [6] He remembered how "she always wore voluminous black clothes sewn with bugles, and out of doors a Queen Victoria bonnet with a black feather and two black ribbons which tied under her chin—and in these she would always be willing to take any number of grandchildren on any number of excursions." [7] This "wonderful grandmother" [8] was a trial to her more conventional children, who were learning too well the respectable behaviour of the best people, because she had little sense of propriety and less of the expected niceties of housekeeping. "Neither her bonnet nor her beads and bugles could disguise her resemblance to the stout old slow-moving Maori woman who would now and then come to our back door

with a flax kit full of kumaras to sell." [9] It is probable that her
tiny but rotund form loomed so large in her grandson's memory,
not overburdened with affection toward his relatives, with the
exception of his King country uncle who became a dominant
influence in his life, because she presented such a complete
contrast to the strict, pious, and respectable people in his immediate surroundings. In her loving-kindness and sympathy to
those who in any way needed help, his grandmother was a
legendary figure in the small township into which she had been
dropped and where she spent twenty years of her life.

On their arrival in the '70's his grandparents, like so many
of the settlers who had been induced to emigrate, possessed
little or nothing; but it was not long before they had been able
to buy land and own the freehold of a storekeeper's shop in the
main street. Twenty years later they were able to retire to an
Auckland suburb, leaving the business they had established to
the oldest of their three children, Frank Sargeson's father.

The father seems to have inherited few of the qualities of
the "wonderful grandmother," who "contrived to make every
moment come vividly alive," [10] and little enough from his own
reasonably successful father, who retired with a modest compe-
tence. The "spiritual buoyancy" of his mother had been diverted
to a fervent but narrow sectarian faith. He was uninterested
in the acquisition of land or property and but little concerned
with the details and activities of storekeeping. When he met
his future wife, she also had been exposed to sectarian influence,
although she had more worldly ideas about the value of money
and middle-class respectability.

She was the oldest of seven children and had been born in
England at Great Yarmouth. Her father was from Holbeach in
the Lincolnshire fen country (at least until recently a relative
of Frank Sargeson was still living close to North Thoresby,
from which place came the Thomas Kendall whose complex
and tragic life in New Zealand became the theme of one of
his plays). Her mother, who in turns of speech betrayed her
Irish upbringing, had come from Belfast, where she and her
husband lived for a couple of years before finally emigrating
to New Zealand. They arrived in Auckland in the late 1870's.

During the depression of the '90's they there experienced some
of the hardships which became familiar to their grandson forty
years later. His grandfather was a painter, decorator, and sign-
writer by trade, and after a period in Taranaki, where he went
in search of work, he brought his wife to live next door to his
eldest daughter and her family in Hamilton. He had never
been well-off and with seven children to feed and clothe he was
unlikely as a tradesman to make more than a modest living in
this land of promise to which he had come.

"He was," wrote his grandson, "a slight figure of a man with
a trim white beard and formal dignified manners, so you knew
immediately that you would be dismissed from his house if
you got up to any skylarking: it was also evident that he was
the head of his own home." [11] Nevertheless, there was a
freedom of speech here, and in his conversation and the stories
he told he would broach all kinds of subjects that in the house
next door were regarded as completely unsuitable, if mentioned
in the presence of children, and were absolutely forbidden.
Like Sargeson's grandparents on his father's side, these two had
forsaken the Church of England, but their grandson records
how deeply he was moved when he surprised his grandfather
reading the Bible which, in spite of the regular family prayers
in his own home, he had never seen his parents reading. As
the old man shut the book he said: "My boy, if we could be
sure that the word of God is revealed in this book none of us
would fear to die." [12] The boy brooded for days over what
seemed to him a strange utterance, but at last came to the
conclusion that his grandfather loved life so intensely that he
had no wish to leave it, an attitude which profoundly affected
him because it was so strikingly different from his own youthful
feeling: "There was scarcely a day when I didn't try to compensate for my own unhappiness, my disgust and perplexity by
morbidly repeating to myself, *It is but a little while. . . .*" [13]

As a young girl his mother had left school to become a pupil-
teacher in Auckland, but before long was working as an as-
sistant in a shop that produced and sold woollen goods. It was
owned by a nonconformist family with whom she frequently
stayed when her own people had left for Taranaki. When a

branch shop was opened in Hamilton the girl accompanied the
owner's sister to look after and develop the new venture. There,
in due course, she married the young storekeeper, who was
not yet thirty; but not for long to remain as a storekeeper's
wife, for within a few years, indeed, shortly after the birth of
the second son, Frank, her husband sold both store and bake-
house. He had spent a year in passing examinations to qualify
himself as a public accountant, and after his retirement from
business became Town Clerk of the small borough of Hamilton
at a salary of £250 a year, which did not tend to increase as
his family grew larger. There were four children, two boys
and two girls. The oldest by four years had what is usually
called a successful career and rose from office boy to General
Manager of a large dairy company. The second, the subject of
this biographical sketch, was born on March 23, 1903, and
judged by the same standards had what is usually called an
unsuccessful career; but because he was able to escape from
the restricting bonds of family and the small-town social life
that hemmed him in, and eventually discover a way of living
in which his talents and personality could function more easily,
he has lived to become a significant figure in New Zealand
literature and a valuable part of its vital and developing tradition.

II   *The Puritan Conscience*

"Puritanism," wrote Jane Mander in *A Story of a New Zealand
River,* "is an awful disease." In boyhood and youth Frank
Sargeson seems to have been exposed to two of its most damaging varieties, both of which still flourish in the New Zealand
of today. His father was completely possessed by an intense
moral fervor that found its expression in a series of negative
commandments: *Thou shalt not* was a more powerful deterrent
than *Thou shalt,* but left little room for any spontaneous enjoyment of life. As with so many nonconformists, it seemed important to him to impress on others not that they must overcome
their temptations, but that they were morally reprobate if they
had any temptations that needed overcoming. He divided his
life between the business of the Borough Council and the busi-

ness of his Church. He was kind in his own manner and charitable within his means, but he was determined to help only responsible and hard-working recipients. His religion was associated with the gospel of work, and only through the Church was it possible to invite the soul. He was a fanatical prohibitionist, a nonsmoker, and an opponent of any form of entertainment that in his opinion might lead to or encourage prurient desires. In after-years his son, who was accustomed to remarks heard from the boys at school that his father was the worst wowser in the town, would suddenly remember the apoplectic purple of his face as he thundered about the absolute necessity of neck-to-knee bathing costumes. Like the parents of Ernest Pontifex in Samuel Butler's *The Way of All Flesh* Sargeson's parents succeeded in conveying the impression that they had always been thoroughly good people, unaffected by the temptations to which far too many of their fellow mortals were prone; and to them sex had become the "dirty little secret" so despised by D. H. Lawrence.

If the father was what Frank Sargeson has called "the pure puritan," the man with a deep, if narrow, religious conviction who would abide by his beliefs even if the whole world opposed him, his mother was an "impure puritan" whose attitude was more closely related to a middle-class protestantism which easily degenerates into an irreligious social conformity. She was perhaps less affected by the word of God than by the word of Man, at least of those men who were able to combine successful business with earthly mansions before they departed for the heavenly ones they would surely inhabit. She was capable of hinting to her children that she might have done better for herself, and showed signs of regret that her husband had turned his back on the claims of property and calls of social advancement. In some matters she was less rigid than he, since she was not so animated by a zeal for moral perfection that he had defined without reference to the imperatives of middle-class respectability.

When Frank Sargeson reviewed Dan Davin's novel, *Roads from Home,* he wrote: "Something very like New Zealand is to be found in astonishing abundance. . . . This sense of reality is due to the fact that the book takes the puritan spirit for granted, puritanism being a major influence on our behaviour." [14] Certainly it was a major influence in the days of his childhood and adolescence and has remained as one of the important themes of his mature writing. That he was able to escape from its dreadful insensitivity to some of the more significant aspects of the experience of living was probably due to an instinctive urge to keep as close as possible to a deeper and more elemental reality than could be found in his immediate environment. He was torn between the life of the spirit as it had been defined and practised by his parents and the life of the senses which he experienced in his many wanderings to and through the back country.

Six or seven miles from Hamilton, not far from the road to Cambridge, lay the farm of his Cornish uncle, to which, packed in their buggy, the whole family was accustomed to make excursions; but it was not until high school days that he began to develop that deep love for the countryside, and particularly its wilder and more inaccessible features, which prepared him for another major influence in his life. This sensitivity to nature is partly concealed in his writing, because there is no self-consciousness, no embarrassing asssertiveness about his treatment of the New Zealand scene. The spirit of place often emerges, but never in the form of that clumsy guidebook lyricism so painfully indulged in by some New Zealand writers. Any description of scene becomes woven into the texture of his characters' thoughts and feelings. In *I Saw in My Dream* it is not for the sake of self-expression, nor for the obtrusive information of his readers, that he writes of

. . . a whole world empty and waiting, with no sound and nothing moving except when the birds flew out. And as he watched Dave was feeling a sort of pull, feeling that he was being more and more urgently invited into this waiting world—that the bush might persist in having its own life, but the cleared land was empty and waiting, helpless to live now a life of its own, and depending instead on some new and mysterious relationship with the lives of men and their beasts. Though it worried him to try to find words for it all—only the feeling of invitation was urgent and clear, and with it a sense of waste, and time and opportunity lost.[15]

In his boyhood this invitation from the more remote and bush-clad hills and streams was felt obscurely in the blood, and as soon as possible he was taking long, and sometimes solitary, excursions by bicycle into the back country, to Te Aroha towards the northeast, to Pirongia Mountain in the southwest and along the Awakino valley to Taranaki in the south. In *Up onto the Roof and Down Again* he suggests that

. . . Te Aroha, pressing forward a little onto the plain, partly detached from the Kaimai range, used to be my favourite climb; from the top I used to see almost the whole of the world that I had so far known and felt. The sweep of the Bay of Plenty was magnificent, and I was fascinated by the sight of places I had never visited—the rounded mount at Tauranga, long and sandy Matakana island, bare of the pines that have now transfigured it into a sort of New Zealand version of the country of the pointed firs. You turned round and looked back over the Hauraki plain, the Waikato plain and valley, with the farms contracted to pocket-handkerchief size, and remembered that from the top of Pirongia, standing up beyond, you had seen the west coast and the Tasman sea: you turned north and looked along the Coromandel peninsula, and over the waters of the gulf as far as Waiheke island: and your eye followed the line of the Kaimais southwards until they broadened out to form the Mamaku plateau—the first great step as it were up onto the roof of the Island. And right until the day I die there will be unpredictable occasions when all of that vast scene will vividly re-create itself for me: my eyes will see something, my ears hear something—it may suddenly be there through any one of my senses.[16]

The spirit of place was invading his puritan conscience, which had been nourished mainly by Bible class and a dangerous insensitivity to the life of the senses. He recalls how, as he climbed Te Aroha, he was always aware that he was following in the footsteps of Christian in *Pilgrim's Progress*, a book that continued to exert an influence on his writing; but when he reached the top of what is known as Bald Spur, "my imagination would immediately begin to work, and I would feel my body tingle."

As he approached the bush "which might have been the hiding-place, the eternal dwelling-place of Apollyon himself, I was secretly terrified," but directly he found himself in the midst of the unspoiled trees and undergrowth:

I would now want to dawdle. My time of delight would be over far too soon—my time of delight in that half-lit place of springing trees and wheeling ferns and swinging vines. It might be Apollyon's world, but it was mine too—and it was as though the devil entered into me. I wanted to kick up my heels and run about, to touch and put my arms about this tree and that, to sniff at handfuls of leaf-mould, to listen for the sounds of birds and running water, to look for the tracks of wild pigs. . . . I am sure that my mouth must have drawn up at the corners, perhaps my ears grew longer. It was the pure life of the senses that I temporarily lived, a pure and shameless life that was suddenly and miraculously permitted me. But only too soon some word or thought was bound to remind me of my pilgrim's role . . . and somewhere at the back of my mind there was always the memory that, after all, it *was* heaven at the top.[17]

There seemed to be an irreconcilable conflict between the pilgrim's role and the life of the senses which, as time went on, included strong sexual desires; yet, whenever the claims of school sports on Saturdays, and church and Bible class on Sundays, were not interfered with, he would seize every opportunity that holidays afforded to escape into this world of delight and freedom.

III   *The Honeysuckle Tree*

Meanwhile he was attending the Hamilton High School; and by his fourth year there, when he was seventeen, he had already begun to study for the Auckland University College extramural examinations in law in order to qualify as a solicitor. It was in the same year that he made his first unaccountably delayed visit to his mother's youngest brother, who now and then had turned up in Hamilton with his belongings round his shoulders and half a sheep in a sack, and as she greeted him with some asperity his sister would ask "what he meant by daring to appear before respectable people looking like a swagger." [18] This unconventional uncle who was to have an abiding influence on the course of his nephew's future life had been a plumber by trade after he left primary school, but in 1913 he had drawn in a Crown Lands ballot 600 acres (O.R.P.—occupation with right of purchase) at the far end of a narrow valley at Okahakura, about seven miles north of Taumaranui in the King Country. To this he had added another 150 acres of freehold Maori land, and although he was unmarried and only sixteen years older than his nephew he had built for himself a five-roomed house with woolshed and orchard, and with incredible industry had cleared and fenced all his land, leaving only a few strips of bush in the steeper parts. In so doing, as he ruefully recognized, he had committed all the mistakes that had been made by hundreds of new settlers with insufficient experience and knowledge of agriculture. He was surrounded by abandoned or soon-to-be abandoned farms where the owners had given up their desperate attempts to establish a stable pasturage and to cope with eroded soil and landslides. By his own strength of will and continual labour he had managed to hold on, although his land was mortgaged and, despite his efforts, always in process of deterioration.

What very quickly fascinated his nephew was not only the remote farm but the character and personality of its owner, who seemed to have been able to come to terms with himself and his isolated surroundings in such a manner that it struck the young man as almost unbelievable and yet strangely disturbing. Nevertheless, on this first of what proved to be many visits, he was more repelled than attracted by the quietly sceptical reception accorded his voluble account of how his Bible class camp had inspired him. He was disconcerted and a little disgusted by the presence of a middle-aged man with a hook instead of a hand who sometimes worked in the district, and more disconcerted by his uncle's later comment: "We're all of us maimed in some way." [19] He was ill at ease, frightened by the silent and forbidding character of the hills that surrounded the farm and secretly wished that he was back at the Bible class camp preparing to lead all people to Christ. However, during visits that became more frequent until he finally left his home

in Hamilton, he found himself pouring into his uncle's ears all
the confusions and complexities of his unsettled adolescence—
his preoccupation with Christian dogma, his dissatisfaction with
the progress of his legal studies, the fragments of information
he had gained from theological and other reading, his sexual
frustrations and his continual circling round the question of
the purpose of his life.

His uncle was a rather silent man who would rarely comment but, instead, carry on with the farmwork on which they
would be both engaged, pausing at times to light his pipe or
to draw attention to some aspect of the natural life around
them. He "was slightly built, with very wide shoulders and
very narrow hips; he was fair-skinned and sharp-featured, with
Scandinavian blue eyes that seemed always to be taking in the
minutest details of everything he looked at. . . . He could handle
any tool, particularly an axe, with a grace and precision that
seemed to elude his muscle-bound neighbours." [20]

In spite of his solitariness and his deafness he gave the impression of being thoroughly contented and at ease and was
always in close communion with living and growing things. To
his nephew, excited and bored by turns, unhappy in his home
and uncertain of his direction, the untroubled poise of his uncle
who was "every moment of the time responding with a quiet
but profound joy to all appearances of created things" [21] was
both an irritation and an unexpected challenge. It was not surprising that before long, as he has recorded:

I had transferred to my uncle and the farm all the affection which
had been previously fixed on the transcendental heaven I had
imagined at the top of Te Aroha mountain. . . . The farm at one and
the same time was a new heaven and a new earth, two separate entities
that were inseparably united: a heaven that was made human by the
presence of my uncle, and an earth that by his presence was transformed into a model of what the human world might be. [22]

Although it is perhaps true to say, especially of the early
sketches which caught the attention of a wide circle of readers,
that Sargeson's writing is more concerned with revealing the
false values of New Zealand society, there are frequent under-

tones that suggest a firmer, more balanced and positive view of life and these stem in large part from his early exposure to a more satisfactory way of living discovered in his varied experiences on the farm of his uncle. On that first visit the youth found almost by accident, and certainly without realizing the significance it would later have for him, a symbol to which he would continually return. It was not only a symbol but the promise of new directions, of an escape from his sectarian entanglements and the career of a law clerk, of a discovery of himself in relation to the land of his birth. In the early morning, as he wondered how he could conveniently beat a rapid retreat from the disturbing atmosphere in which he found himself, he asked the name of a large tree that dominated the skyline on a high ridge nearby. The reply he received startled him. It was a honeysuckle, not of course the introduced English variety which reminded exiled settlers of what they called Home, but a great New Zealand tree. As the years passed the tree, the farm, his uncle became for him symbols of a new world that he had been slowly discovering in the New World, symbols of a New Zealander's pilgrimage through life that, still without much sense of direction, he was nevertheless beginning to undertake. When after his uncle's death in 1948 he wrote *Up onto the Roof and Down Again* he recalled how in moods of depression he had regarded his uncle as the only *civilized* person in New Zealand, adding:

At least he was something for me to hang on to. Instead of my uncle's image it was a general image of the farm and its surrounding country that would most persistently suggest itself to my mind; and if there *was* anything particular about this image it was the great honeysuckle tree.[23]

At the age of seventeen, when his uncle had told him the name by which this tree was known, he had little idea of the significance it would assume in future years. Passing over the Mamaku Heights at twilight some time after his uncle's death he saw from the window of the Waikato bus a scene of desolation, not altogether unfamiliar to New Zealanders; but in its midst "the tall and feathery shape of a tree, clear against the

sky on the not-so-distant horizon . . . for me standing not for
New Zealand as it is, but *New Zealand as it might worthily
have been.*" [24]

Until he met his uncle on the farm that was to become his
place of refuge and in some ways his source of inspiration, he
had had no access to standards of value other than those he
had experienced in his home; but he had developed a rather
unusual interest in theological disputation, and his reading of
Milton interfered seriously with his study for law examinations.
Quarrels with his parents became more frequent and he enjoyed
irritating his father by reminding him that towards the end of
his life John Wesley had rejected the idea that Methodists
should leave the Church of England and had believed that if
they did God would leave *them.* It was only a matter of time
before the almost inevitable break came. Meanwhile he had
been reading Pascal:

When I discovered that Pascal had written that nature is only the
first custom, as custom is second nature; and that there is nothing
man may not make natural, nor anything natural he may not lose, I
was able to see that the environment which my father and mother
took for granted, and which was for them a natural reality nothing
could alter and nobody could question, needn't necessarily be what it
was at all: I could for example imagine that it might be much more
the sort of life which my uncle lived on his farm.[25]

He was working in a law office in Hamilton, and relieving his
increasing tension by playing strenuous games of hockey, when
at Easter in 1925 he made the last of a number of visits to his
uncle who, after listening to his flow of grievances, suggested
that he should live at the farm and help in the afternoons,
leaving the rest of the day for his study. He accepted with
alacrity, but it was four and a half years before he saw his
uncle again. Only a fortnight after his return home, intending
to resign from his office position, a quarrel with his mother
developed to such a pitch that he left the house forever, but
instead of going to his uncle's he went to Auckland, threw himself into his studies and finally was admitted as solicitor early
in 1926. For a brief period he worked in a law office in Auckland;
and then, in February, 1927, left for England.

CHAPTER 2

The Making of a Writer

*"New Zealand literature has had two tragedies—the first was
Katherine Mansfield, and the second is Frank Sargeson."*

ANON.

I Solitary Pilgrimage

Frank Sargeson was to say many years later that, like so many
of his fellow countrymen, he had to visit Europe to discover
that he was a New Zealander. Nevertheless, at this time, a little
before his twenty-fourth birthday, it was not apparent that the
recently qualified solicitor was either travelling in the right
direction or intent on any more important form of discovery
than that which would lead Robin Hyde to call one of her last
novels "The Godwits Fly" (1938). He had broken away from
his family and the Waikato environment where he had been
born and come to manhood. He had been able to save very
little money, and what he had saved was mostly derived from
the sale of a section of land left to him by his grandmother.
He had no future to which he could look forward with any
satisfaction, for the routine of a small-town lawyer was not one
that offered any promise of answering the questions that bothered
him. If he had escaped temporarily from the provincial setting,
the Bible-class camps and the narrow confines of a rigid and
sectarian family, he had not even made the attempt to return
to his uncle and the glimpse of a life to which he had been
strongly attracted.

As yet he had given no indication that he possessed creative
ability to any marked degree, although he had known that he
was fascinated by the world of sense and by his uncle's keenness
of response to "all appearances of created things." An early

27

impulse to express himself on paper had been as unproductive as it was ludicrous. After reading Scott's *Ivanhoe* at the age of twelve he had been seized with a desire to write, to which he had responded by attempting to transcribe the whole novel into a school exercise book, a proceeding discovered by his mother and mercilessly ridiculed. In his immediate surroundings there had been no stimulus towards creativeness and, although he had been encouraged to join the local Shakespeare club, almost his only outlet had been in long excursions and in sport, particularly hockey and tennis, showing outstanding skill in the latter. On visits to the King Country farm he had been disconcerted to discover that his uncle, with only a primary-school education, was in the habit of reading the books scattered about on the chairs and shelves of his house, books heard of or 'studied' by his nephew but never read. He could not remember his parents ever going out together in the evening except to church, and he knew that his father had attended not more than two or three stage performances in his life. Even library books were frequently condemned in his household as "unclean"; and yet the growing boy who had seen himself as Christian in *Pilgrim's Progress* had before long, and after increasing association with his uncle, become conscious of the wish "to achieve something in some way related to the fruit hanging on the trees" [1] in the orchard where both of them had sometimes worked together. He had an ill-defined desire to escape into an unknown and presumably freer world, to find himself, to explore his own relation to a larger environment and to an older tradition; and the answers to the questions he was continually asking could not be found, he knew, in the Hamilton of his boyhood.

By no stretch of the imagination could the New Zealand he was leaving be regarded as a place that could easily provide intellectual, spiritual, or aesthetic nutriment. From 1912 to 1925 its Prime Minister had been William Massey, in many ways a typical representative of current New Zealand attitudes, an Auckland farmer, a Presbyterian from Ulster, who looked upon his country as the Empire's outlying farm. A.R.D. Fairburn was to write in his poem, *Dominion*, published in 1938:

> we have prospered greatly,
> we, the destined race, rulers of conquered isles,
> sprouting like bulbs in warm darkness, putting out
> white shoots under the wet sack of Empire.[2]

And already in 1924, not long before Sargeson left for England, the young poet R. A. K. Mason had written in his *Sonnet of Brotherhood:*

> what
> of these beleaguered victims this our race
> betrayed alike by Fate's gigantic plot
> here in this far-pitched perilous hostile place
> this solitary hard-assaulted spot
> fixed at the friendless outer edge of space.[3]

Frank Sargeson himself was later to say in a comment on Sherwood Andreson, whom he greatly admired: "It is a pity that [his] work is not better known in New Zealand. Anderson has lived his life in an environment similar to our own, raw, aesthetically hostile." [4] Fourteen years after Sargeson's return to Auckland, Anna Kavan, writing in *Horizon,* described one of New Zealand's cities, not perhaps without malice, but also not without truth as "indeterminate."

It isn't New Zealand and it isn't anywhere else. It's null, it's dull, it's tepid, it's mediocre and the downunder of the spirit. The houses are drowsing, the leaves are falling, the flies are circling; trucks full of sheep's carcasses clatter drearily over the railway bridge, the fire-screen worked by the wife of an early settler moulders in the museum.[5]

This was probably not all that Frank Sargeson saw, but there was enough resemblance to the reality he had experienced to account partly for his determination to see the land of his ancestors and to make the return pilgrimage on which they came.

The New Zealand between two wars had advanced well beyond the pioneering stage; but it was still a land where people talked of Home, meaning England, where farmers and townsmen alike tended to be provincial in attitude and either overassertive

or on the defensive, where the anticipated characteristics of what
was called 'a young country' were displayed in other people's
wars and on the football field rather than in qualities of the
mind and the exploration of life, where land speculation was
rife and, to use the words of the Australian poet, Bernard
O'Dowd, there was "all old sin in full malignant flower." [6] Significantly enough, in the first published collection of New Zealand short stories, its compiler, O. N. Gillespie, wrote in 1930:

Throughout the hundred years of New Zealand's history, one purpose
has dominated our people. They sought, and still seek, to refashion
in these islands the homeland they had left. Here and there a more
daring dreamer hoped to make the copy better than the original.

The small boy, Frank Sargeson, was not so different in his
aim when he began with great labour to copy out the whole of
Ivanhoe. The young lawyer, Frank Sargeson, as he stepped on
to English soil had begun another pilgrimage which would in
due course bring him back to New Zealand; but it would be
long before the true significance of the great honeysuckle tree
could enter into his consciousness, long before he would even
begin to discover some of the outlines of social life in New
Zealand, longer still before he would be able to find the words
and rhythms of prose in which to describe them.

It was a solitary pilgrimage. The distance from a lodging
house in Auckland to a lodging house in Bloomsbury, in Paris,
Berne, Genoa, or Florence was not to be measured in miles but
in terms of centuries of civilization and the weight of tradition.
If he had felt at home in the wildest and most remote areas of
the Waikato and Taranaki, he now felt solitary in crowded cities
and in country districts where the villages were never far apart.
This was no Grand Tour of the son of an English gentleman,
but a makeshift journey, rucksack on back, of a small-town New
Zealander, accustomed to primitive conditions, to farm life, to
finding his way and roughing it in the bush. Although he had
his share of personal and erotic adventures and picked up much
passing and casual company, he remained something of a displaced person wherever he went, whether he was walking in

Devon or Cornwall or whether he took his rucksack from Paris to Strasbourg and by way of Switzerland to the edge of the Lombardy plain.

Much of his time, however, was spent in London working through the plans and charts which he had devised in the vain but determined attempt to catch up on centuries of civilization in a few months. It was not that he had succumbed to the besetting sin of the New Zealander, filled with the expectation that in the cities of Europe he would find himself in the midst of all intellectual endeavour and at the crossways of all artistic achievement. On the contrary, in many ways he found the old world oppressive. It weighed his spirit down with the pressure of countless generations and, although he sometimes imagined that he would be able to adjust himself to the completely new conditions and was attracted by much of its artistic sophistication, the ever-present image of his uncle or the farm would reveal to him that quite unexpectedly he belonged to the new world rather than the old. This feeling was intensified in Switzerland where, contrary to his anticipations, he found that never for long was he out of sight of people; even here he missed those demands on individual resourcefulness which were always present in the wilds of New Zealand. The solitary wild honeysuckle tree returned again and again to his mind, and in later years he made scarcely any use of the Continental or English scene and its people in the stories he wrote. Only in one, *An Englishwoman Abroad,* does he make any effort to recreate a small piazza and its open air cafe where the masculine narrator picks up two separate acquaintanceships with an Englishwoman of doubtful reputation and two equally doubtful girls from Marseilles; yet even in this story one of the minor themes is antagonism and a failure to adjust. The French girls, pleasant and talkative, despised Italians and despised the Englishwoman more; and she in the presence of the narrator would cry a little as she remembered how she used to sing in the choir in her parish church.

It was not only lack of money that would send Sargeson back to New Zealand; it was a considered preference for the country which had become part of himself. Even if, as he thought, his uncle was the only civilized person there, it was the excitement and the uncertain promise of the new to which he was still attracted. Nor did he make any effort to earn money while in England. He neither attempted to pursue his legal studies nor did he seek any position, legal or otherwise. Instead he occupied himself with his extraordinary and complicated charts to which he was always referring, charts headed literature, with subheadings of poetry, fiction, history, philosophy, charts concerned with music and the theatre, with architecture and science. He tended to consider that any time spent in not advancing his knowledge by reading in the British Museum was time wasted. Commenting later on this youthful extravagance, he found it not only rather absurd but indicative of an arrogance and an incapacity to understand his own limitations. His endeavours were certainly naive, but he admitted to himself that, although his quest was in part an attempt to discover how the best minds had come to terms with their environment, it also had as its aim a comparison of his own knowledge of human behaviour which, in his innocence, he thought profound, with that of the great minds of the past.

It was only during the last period of his stay in London that in the seclusion of his Bloomsbury boarding house he began to write; but what he wrote, indubitably his own, he soon recognized was not of a much higher level than his earlier attempt to transcribe a whole novel. This time, as he has recorded in a radio talk, he began to set down as accurately as he could remember everything that had happened to himself. His manuscript was centred on the well-worn theme of the growth of a young man, and its model was, of course, Joyce's *A Portrait of the Artist as a Young Man;* but unfortunately the New Zealand writer was under the illusion that all that was necessary in order to create an interesting and valuable book was an accurate memory, which he knew he possessed. To his surprise he found that he had the greatest difficulty in selecting the significant material. To his greater surprise he discovered that his facility with language was insufficient to cope with the most ordinary situation. It was in this mood, oppressed by his failure to write anything that even he considered readable, oppressed by the number of books that he would be unable to read, oppressed by the weight of what seemed in any real sense to be an alien tradition, that he returned to New Zealand in the early months of 1928.

II *Return and Depression*

He had succeeded in nothing. His pilgrimage seemed to have been a false start towards an unknown destination; his dedication to writing a passing whim or a vague aspiration rather than a confident gesture. He appeared to be no closer to the answers to those questions which had worried him through adolescence and youth, to the problem of WAIAMIHEA. In *A Portrait of the Artist* Stephen Dedalus had determined to fly by the nets of nationality, language, and religion in order to become the artificer; but Sargeson had held fast to no such creed. He had not even escaped completely from his family; nor could he comfort himself with any claim that he had within him what it takes to become a creative writer. He had nearly convinced himself that he had returned because of all that he thought his uncle represented for him, but he made no attempt to go to Okahakura. Instead, he made his way home to face not only the curiosity and complaints of his mother about how he had spent his time and money, but also his own despair that he had failed in his quest for self-realization. If he had learnt anything during his year's absence, it was incommunicable to those around him; and yet, after he had overcome his deep depression he felt more than ever convinced that what he had done was right for him. He borrowed a pound from his brother and went to Auckland to look for work in newspaper and law offices, boldly pretending that his stay overseas had increased his qualifications for journalism or for legal practice. The position he found, however, was one for which he had applied by letter. In June, 1928 he was actively engaged in the routine work of a government department in Wellington.

For a few weeks it looked as if he had at last taken his mother's advice and 'pulled himself together.' He was becoming a model office worker, interested in his tasks and anxious to improve his efficiency by overtime at his desk. In one of the stories he wrote much later, he described two old men concerned with stationery and files in the basement of a large government department:

They were called the two old duds because years ago they'd had
every opportunity to learn the knack of writing minutes on files, and
they never had. Instead they'd turned out duds. Here they were
getting on to be old men, and all they did was look after the stationery. While upstairs quite young men were writing minutes on
files, and doing it so well they had chances of a future. In years to
come they'd be so high up they'd have to go to the opening of
Parliament.[7]

Sargeson has recorded elsewhere[8] that he was saved from such
a dismal fate, from mistaking "a social hell" for heaven, by an
incident that occurred when with his companions he was drinking at a hotel bar. A bedraggled and dirty social outcast appeared among the drinkers and after looking each one in the face
had announced with belligerent conviction that John Keats was
the greatest poet who had ever lived. After a little hesitation
someone had asked the seedy intruder if he also was a poet, but
Sargeson, feeling something more was required, observed that
that perhaps he was right about Keats. Instead of the pleased
recognition of a kindred spirit, he was surprised and humiliated
by a violent push on the face from the eccentric who, after he
had been led away, continued to announce in various corners
of the crowded bar that John Keats was the greatest poet who
had ever lived.

This slightly ridiculous episode had more than a passing effect
on the young man's mind and emotions. Instead of dismissing it
as an odd and probably irrational gesture of a partly demented
man, he brooded over its meaning and imagined he saw in it a
defiant if ineffectual protest against the sordid values of a society that found no place for anything outside the routine of
suburb and office. He was aroused from his torpid state of respectable conventionality and turned with mounting enthusiasm
to his Keats by whose poetry he was brought to such a state of
enthusiasm that he was soon sitting up late into the night com-
posing odes and narrative poems. It surprised and exhilarated
him to discover that he could write with facility, until he noticed
that he was mingling the pagan and medieval worlds with reckless abandon; once more he was overcome with a sense of futility
and self-contempt. Nevertheless, he continued to read Keats and

before long came across a passage in his letters which simply and vividly described an old Scottish woman being carried in a chair. Once again he was seized with a fit of enthusiasm because Keats had observed that he wondered what the life of this woman had been.

I was moved at last to such a state of heart-knocking excitement that I felt driven from my room to the streets outside: I walked for hours which I was never afterwards likely to forget—because I began with the thought that the wonderful poet the world had received could hardly be reckoned a gift, when he had had to be paid for by the loss of a novelist who might have been reckoned no less wonderful; and I returned home with the conviction that I was going to repair the loss by writing the sort of novels that John Keats might have written. It was a belief that sustained me for nearly a year.[9]

During this period he wrote four stories which, although they were never published, were considerably in advance, he thought, of anything he had written previously, if only for the reason that he was making the attempt to deal with the possible crises in the lives of some elderly clerks, and therefore was forced to rely on his sympathetic imagination. His continual bouts of exaltation and acute depression were signs of the nervous tension from which he was unable to free himself. His eyes troubled him and headaches kept recurring. He was worried by his neglect of his office work, and his writing was punctuated by a series of street adventures and in particular, by a close companionship with a friend whom he encountered in the library where he was accustomed to read and write. Strangely enough this friend reminded him of his uncle and had the same imperturbable independence and carefree manner of living, spending his time between his home, the library and his place of work as a cleaner in a large store. It was this friend who advised him to find a way of life which would enable him to pursue his writing without the constant pressure of a respectable position; but it was still not easy for the young man, brought up in a household where evangelical piety had been equated with the gospel of work, to make a clear break with the past.

Nevertheless, in another mood of depression and with the holidays approaching, he decided at last to visit his uncle. He

did not return to his government work, and, although at this
time he was in a state that amounted to one of nervous prostration he never again sought to live the conventional life of the
seeker after bourgeois respectability. From this September, 1929,
he would have to face a repetition of those questions to which
he referred over twenty years later when he wrote in *Landfall:*

Why don't I write detective/adventure/love stories? Why don't I
write descriptive articles about my travels for newspapers and maga-
zines? Why don't I write about people who live in state houses? Why
don't I write stories with a plot? Why don't I write about decent
people? Why don't I look on my writing as just a hobby? Why do I
read all that dry stuff? Why don't I get myself a job? Why don't I
realize I must earn a proper living the same as other people? Why
don't I leave off living as though the slump is still on? Why don't I
accept my responsibilities? Why with my brain don't I take up school-
teaching or go into business? Why don't I grow up? Why don't I
wake up and stop dreaming? Why don't I accept the world as it is?
Why don't I keep proper hours? Why is my garden so untidy when
I spend so much time in it? Why don't I learn to behave myself?
Why do I associate with riff-raff who never have a penny to bless
themselves with any more than I have? Why do I stay in New Zealand if I want to make my name? Why must I always think myself
different? Why do I answer back with quotations out of the Bible
when I have left off going to church and haven't a spark of religion
in me? Why am I always joking? Why do I persist in being cheerful
over serious matters? Why don't I realize I am a disgrace? Why do
I suppose I know better than other people? Why am I such a mass
of ignorance? Why do I waste so much time? Why don't I get out
and mix with people? Why have I lost interest in politics? Why
aren't I ashamed of my wasted life?[10]

It was in a state of extraordinary excitement and exhilaration
that he walked along the river valley to his uncle's farm at
Okahakura, almost four and a half years since he had seen it.
As he saw the once familiar surroundings and stood in the
orchard where he had told his uncle that he wanted to be like
him, he experienced a few moments of what he has called "hal-
lucinated vision." His absent uncle was there with his scythe;
early spring had changed into summer, and "I was listening as
I had listened previously for those sounds which might reveal to

me the secrets of all creation." [11] Whatever the passing experience might mean, it left him with the conviction that he had discovered without any possible doubt at all what the purpose of his life must be as long as it lasted.

He stayed with his uncle until May, 1931, when he moved to the seaside bach at Takapuna on Auckland's north shore, where he had lived for a short period before going abroad; but until his uncle died in 1948 he continued to make regular visits to the farm. In the full sense of the word he had at last come home. WAIAMIHEA no longer bothered him as it had done formerly. His manner of settling down had been very different from that advised by his relatives and practised by so many of his Hamilton associates. He had temporarily adopted the idea, first suggested by his uncle, of helping on the farm for a part of each day and spending as much time as was available at his studies. Now his studies were not at all concerned with legal problems but with the problems of writing the novel on which his mind was set. In this way he recovered his health and devoted himself to the exploration of the craft of writing, a craft that would remain his constant preoccupation.

It was to this period of his apprenticeship that he referred when much later he gave a broadcast on "Writing a Novel," and later still in his contribution to the series called "Beginnings" in the literary quarterly, *Landfall*. Deeply embedded in his mind he had retained the memory of a young girl to whom he had been strongly attracted in his Hamilton schooldays. This girl in her small-town setting became the starting point for the theme of a novel which absorbed him for more than a year. When it was finished it was sent off to the publisher, Jonathan Cape, whose reader then was Edward Garnett. Alterations were suggested and the typescript was returned "when the gold standard was abandoned in 1931." [12] It was never published, but the author's critical instinct had already led him to the conclusion that the book was a failure in comparison with the work he wished to accomplish, and more especially he was dissatisfied with what he called the Galsworthian prose in which it was written. If he had escaped from the naive habit of imitating, he had not yet achieved something unmistakably his own and emanating from the New Zealand scene.

Living by himself once again at Takapuna, Sargeson was forced to join the growing army of the unemployed. He was faced with the task not so much of earning a living as of existing, while he concerned himself with the problems of writing and with the New Zealand that was now sinking into the depths of the great economic depression. For several years the prices for the primary products which supported New Zealanders had been dangerously uneven; employment had not been easy to obtain and the reckless policy of borrowing had resulted in more than a quarter of New Zealand's exports having to be used to pay the interest on loans. In the middle of the world-wide depression, the New Zealand government could think of no better expedient than to attempt to balance the budget by reducing expenditure on public works and the public service, on health, pensions, and education. Unemployment continued to rise towards the figure of 80,000, and a pitiful dole was paid to men who were set to work on useless and unproductive labour. Sargeson himself was receiving nine shillings a week, which at times he was able to increase to fifteen or seventeen shillings by a variety of odd and casual jobs—gardening, labouring and working in kitchens.

Soon the short stories he was beginning to write with growing sureness of touch bore the imprint of those experiences and hardships he shared with thousands of New Zealanders who lived in a country that was supposed to be a working-man's paradise. In *An Attempt at an Explanation,* for example, the small son of a poor seamstress tries to utter the tangled thoughts that were turning over and over in his mind:

I don't know that I can explain it even now, but I know I wasn't crying just because of myself personally. I think it was because for the first time in my life I understood how different sorts of things are all connected up together. I thought of the way my silkworms ate the mulberry leaves that I gave them, and the way the lice had crouched down and held on tight to my hand when I tried to shake them off. And there, right in front of me, the birds were looking for food, and the worms that themselves wanted something to eat were being eaten by the blackbirds. And there came into my heart a pity for all living things that were hungry and needed food.[13]

III   *An Appropriate Language*

What Sargeson was chiefly concerned with, since the time
when he had recognized that the manner in which he had
written his unpublished novel had been derived from an alien
tradition, was the problem of language. He had begun to ask
those questions, the answers to which, if found, would result in
the discovery of the rhythms of speech that might belong to a
young but developing native tradition. Was there

an appropriate language to deal with the material of New Zealand
life? . . . Was language merely the tool the novelist worked with,
or was it a part of the raw material of life he worked upon, or was
it a complex and difficult combination of both? If language was only
a tool, then the less attention it attracted to itself the better; and all
fine writing and delight in words and sentences for their own sake
had better be done without. But things of that kind might very well
be permitted if language was a part of the raw material. Then again,
should it be the aim of the novelist to make the reader see . . . or
should one aim at writing sentences which appealed more to the
reader's ear, making him hear voices as it were—the voice of the
novelist perhaps; the voices of his characters certainly, each with its
own rhythm and cadence? Or should there be an effective blending
of both seeing and hearing?[14]

These were questions that past New Zealand authors had failed
to ask and few even of Sargeson's contemporaries were asking.
Nevertheless, and partly owing to his influence, it was not long
before some of the younger and as yet unknown experimenters
were becoming far more aware that the craft of writing was
not as simple as some of their predecessors had imagined. It
was not something that could be adopted ready-made from the
practice of competent writers, past or present, if they belonged,
as they always did belong, to a part of the world where language was the expression of different social relations and attitudes, however fine those differences might seem to be.

It is only when the craftsman becomes thoroughly involved
with his medium that he is able to control and shape his
thoughts in order to reveal those fragments of the complex human scene that appear to him significant. Because Sargeson was
at first possessed with the idea of the importance of language

through which his impressions of life must be communicated, he discovered that he was beginning to write in a manner completely different from any he had formerly achieved. He was beginning to create. He was finding a new voice, a voice which was at one and the same time individual and typical, which harmonized with the material which was becoming more and more part of his life. These sketches that he was writing first appeared in the pages of a New Zealand periodical which had been founded in 1934 in Christchurch. One of the obstacles with which a New Zealand writer was faced was the difficulty of finding any literary medium, other than the usual assortment of daily newspapers or weekly editions, in which his work would be published. When *Tomorrow* appeared towards the end of the Depression, although it was largely concerned with leftwing politics and was unable to pay contributors, it provided an outlet for some of the younger writers. It was edited by Kennaway Henderson, a water-colourist and cartoonist, and with him was associated a varied assortment of university men, political and other writers, and trade unionists. Those who were connected with the voluntary editorial work of this new journal can still remember the excitement caused by what became a stream of short manuscripts above the signature of an unknown writer, Frank Sargeson. Between March, 1935 and December, 1939 over forty sketches and essays were published, and his first collection of short pieces, *Conversation with My Uncle and Other Sketches*, was issued by the Unicorn Press, Auckland, in 1936. A second collection, *A Man and His Wife*, was in preparation for the Caxton Press, Christchurch, and appeared in 1940.

During this period Sargeson had by no means given up the idea of writing a novel, but after his near miss with Jonathan Cape, after his initial struggles with problems of language, he had found that there were further and more unexpected problems that forced themselves on his attention. The questions with which he was now concerned might be described as extensions of those personal questions which had troubled him as a young man. If at one time he had been striving to discover his own identity and to establish for himself a way of life which would give meaning to his existence, now, in his meditations on a possible hero for the novel he was still determined to write, he was intent on discovering the identity of a New Zealander and what gave meaning to *his* existence. If at one time he had felt that language was part of the raw material of life and that since there was no adequate language at his disposal he must try to create one, now he began to feel that the absence of an established native tradition also affected character, attitude, scene, and incident, and that there were many questions to which he must try to find answers before he could advance further.

In very different circumstances and for very different reasons Joyce Cary in England had come to the conclusion that it was necessary for him to formulate his beliefs before he could write a novel that would satisfy him. Sargeson's particular problems did not exist in England because social and literary traditions had developed over a long period, so that assumptions could be made by novelists and accepted by readers. In New Zealand there were no such traditions and no such assumptions could be made. New Zealanders were still self-conscious or uncertain about being New Zealanders, because they had not yet been made articulate in a literature that had stood the test of time. Even place-names could not be taken for granted as they could in older countries; and the reading public, necessarily accustomed to English literature, had been unable and perhaps unwilling to develop a critical appreciation of work produced in New Zealand.

The problems of tradition were even more complex than might be supposed and, as Sargeson has recorded, he began to ask other questions:

What was the European doing in this country anyway? Had he the right to be here? What were the ideas and ways of life he had brought with him, and how had they developed? Was a society being built which could continue to flourish, or was the European's occupation of the country a kind of tenancy which would eventually be terminated? Did I personally agree with the prevailing sentiments about these matters?[15]

These were questions that concerned the quality of New Zealand life and seemed to imply that the creative writer was not merely a competent photographer of scene and character, but a critical explorer of the lives and attitudes of his fellow countrymen; not

of course a philosopher or sociologist disguising his findings in
fiction, but a writer of narratives revealing habitual modes of
thought and ways of life by a careful use of the material he
chose to examine. Such a writer must necessarily take into account the slight deviations from social and moral standards inherited from the British tradition. Important among these deviations was the puritanism from which in an extreme form Sargeson himself had suffered in his youth.

A few writers, notably Bill Pearson in his "Fretful Sleepers—
a sketch of New Zealand behaviour and its implications for the
artist," [16] have attempted to explore the New Zealander's peculiar
brand of conformity, egalitarianism and self-consciousness. Such
attempts, as they would be the first to admit, are surrounded
with pitfalls and may easily lead to inadequate generalizations
and false conclusions. Nevertheless, they have recognized the
New Zealander's suspicion of variants from an unenlightened
middle-class norm, his conviction that anything worth doing has
monetary implications, his embarrassment at any display of personal feelings, and his assumption that the only valid dream is
one of social security from birth to death. They have noted the
atmosphere of boredom and somnolence, the spiritual deadness
of suburb and country town, relieved only by crude attitudes to
sex, alcohol, and sport, the way in which morality and religion
tend to be equated with public opinion and the curious blend
of docility and independence.

It was the New Zealand variety of such characteristics, ad-
mittedly not unfamiliar throughout the Western world, with
which Sargeson was trying to come to terms. He was finding
that it was necessary to enter "the destructive element" with
human sympathy and understanding in order to create from the
material of observed life a fictional pattern that would reveal
how his fellow countrymen lived and, by implication, how they
might live. For some time he had been reading not only every
New Zealand novel on which he could lay his hands, but also
had been re-reading those novels by writers in other countries
who had experience of some of the problems with which he
found himself struggling. He was drawn to Hawthorne, to Mark
Twain, and to Sherwood Anderson in America, to Lawson in
Australia and to Olive Schreiner in South Africa, and discovered

that in varying ways they had achieved something parallel to what he hoped he might achieve in New Zealand. Although he sometimes found himself humbled by what had been produced elsewhere, he had no intention of giving up the work which had come to mean so much to him. The symbol of the wild honey-suckle tree had not been forgotten, nor the uncertain promise of a new world developing in New Zealand which had filled his thoughts when he was in Switzerland. "After so many years" he wrote in "Beginnings," "I felt I would be left without any aim or purpose in life at all if I abandoned my writing." He has never abandoned it; and therefore in 1953 his fellow writers honoured him with the remarks quoted earlier: "Your work has had, in the past twenty years a liberating influence on the litera-ture of this country. . . . It is not often that a writer can be said to have become a symbol in his own time."

CHAPTER 3

The World of Frank Sargeson

"A sad and savage world."

DAN DAVIN

I   Imaginative Realism

THE SHORT stories of Frank Sargeson should not be considered as a series of unrelated fragments, a haphazard collection of isolated incidents and episodes. Their effect is cumulative like those of the acknowledged masters of the medium, and such is their consistency of tone and their moral coherence that it is possible to speak of a "Sargeson world." This achievement, unequalled by any other New Zealand writer, implies a creative ability that is not confined to the invention of character and selection of material, but is concerned with the imaginative rendering of a moral climate in which the characters move and have their being. The Chekhovian world of the short story, like the Dickensian world of the novel, becomes impressive not because character and incident are startling or exceptional, but because they are seen through the eyes of one who as artist and as man has been able to identify himself with and submerge himself in a world that has its own morality and its own values. Such a writer becomes an imaginative realist, and his writing, whatever its nature, is related to what we usually call poetry, because the moral consistency, the verbal consistency, the unity of tone, of character, and incident combine to give the whole communication.

The writer of short stories is forced to create his own medium. Nothing, not even length, is predetermined for him. Everything depends on the way in which he is able to mould it to serve his purposes. The short story may be merely a compressed narrative, a clearing house for pieces unassimilated into a projected novel. It may be a fable or a parable; it may dispense with plot and seek to evoke a mood, reveal an aspect of character or a contrast in temperaments. It may be an expanded episode or a meditation on an incident. Everything is grist to its mill; but the fineness of its texture is related to the artistic vision that creates it and to the artistic practice that moulds it for ends that are not always immediately perceived by the reader. Its flexibility is its greatest attraction, but at the same time provides a challenge which only the writer who is certain in his aim can afford to accept.

Sargeson's stories are seldom more than two thousand words in length. The longest, *An Affair of the Heart, A Great Day, A Man of Good Will,* and *The Colonel's Daughter,* do not greatly exceed three thousand; and the shorter ones, like *Park Seat, Cats by the Tail, A Piece of Yellow Soap,* or *Chaucerian,* do not extend beyond a few hundred. That is to say, he is a writer whose every word tells, who pays attention to every detail of his work, and does this without in any way emphasizing the manner at the expense of the matter. It is the manner combined with the matter that provides the complete communication. Sargeson is a writer whose art is the art of compression, of contraction rather than expansion, of pruning—not of padding. He gains his effects not by dramatic action or trick endings, by complex characterization or complicated intrigue, for which his practice of brevity offers little opportunity, but by the subtle interplay between the attitude of the narrator and the attitudes of the characters to a small incident or episode. The meaning of a Sargeson story very often lies within the triangle formed by narrator, characters, and reader; but there is a larger meaning that becomes apparent only when the single stories are seen within the framework of the New Zealand setting, and the revelation of and commentary on New Zealand life are recognized as essential elements of the whole Sargeson world of imaginative realism.

At the time when the earlier stories were being published this larger meaning was not available to readers; and even if it had been New Zealand criticism was still suffering from some of the same disabilities and inadequacies affecting creative writing. Chief among these was the inevitable absence of a critical tradition that could do more than direct attention back to an overseas literature, and therefore away from the problems of literature

and criticism in New Zealand. Sargeson has himself suggested
that "the reviewer is a man who spends much of his time seeing
life through the printed pages of a book and if he is a New
Zealand reviewer, the life seen is not very often New Zealand
life." [1] The efforts of the more responsible book reviewers and
critics have generally been in the direction of maintaining critical standards, but too frequently their labours have degenerated
into what an Australian critic has called "the cultural cringe," [2]
a subservience to merely formal conventions and fashions that
have originated in other places and at other times; and the con-
sequent inability to accept New Zealand writing as necessarily
experimental and New Zealand life as its essential raw material.
Too often there has been a tacit acceptance of the kind of writing parodied by Sargeson in a series of sketches published under
the title of "A New Zealand Anthology" in 1937. In a brief
explanation he wrote ironically, "The examples I have chosen
show, I think, the very marrow of the language for which names
have become justly famous." [3] One of them was called "Spur
of Moment":

Working on the wharves Andrew saw life in the raw—sweat and
poverty and dirt, foul language and coarse habits, but fortunately
there were other things. Even these degraded men had their virtues.
Now, if they had had the advantage of a College education! Andrew
thought wistfully of the happy days that were past—the boys with
their upturned faces in the smile of the morning—the cheerful tasks
of scholarship, and football in the honey-coloured end of the afternoon.
What splendid fellows they had all been! Neither by coarse words nor
foul habits had any of them defiled the temple. At night they slept
the deep and satisfying sleep of athletes with clear consciences. He
thought of Paul Wilders, the fleet-footed wing-threequarter, a beautiful figure of flying speed—his swerve had been a thing of stainless
glory. He had been—and still was—Andrew's closest friend, the
cleanest-limbed and highest-minded of them all. . . .[4]

Sargeson was not alone in recognizing that the failure to look
with New Zealand eyes at the raw material of New Zealand life
could only develop and accentuate "the cultural cringe." Nevertheless, many of New Zealand's better critics were becoming
more preoccupied with generalizations about national character-

istics and the attempt to evaluate a tradition that had scarcely
come into existence, than with the exploration of meaning and
experiment in the few New Zealand writers who were beginning
to emerge. They were already engaged in writing histories and
surveys of New Zealand literature, in anthologizing before there
was sufficient material from which to select, fastening their attention on the geographical accidents of isolation, the influences
of mountains, sea, and bush, empty of European tradition, and
the way in which poets and prose writers supported their con-
tentions. They were less ready to examine the relation between
the local environment and Western man's environment in the
twentieth century, or to explore the intellectual and moral climate in which the predicament of a New Zealander might be
seen as a local variation on the predicament of Western man—
to see New Zealand writers against the background of their
local problems as well as in the wider context of human society.
As has been indicated earlier, the questions that Sargeson was
asking made it likely that his work, the work of a dedicated
New Zealand writer, should be read in this wider context. The
questions he was asking, ones not confined to provincial or local
attitudes, would dictate those aspects of New Zealand life which
would absorb his attention. His experiences as a New Zealander
would give reality and energy to those aspects, and his experiments with language and the flexible medium of the short story
would help to provide the pattern, the shape into which his
vision of life would fall. It is therefore the Sargeson world as
revealed in his forty-odd published short stories to which it is
first necessary to turn.

It is not a densely populated world, inhabited mainly by the
waifs and strays of civilization, the outsiders, the displaced
people and social outcasts, by the lonely and inarticulate, the
seasonal and itinerant workers. They are 'fringe' characters who
tend to be isolated from the community, who take no part in
the activities of organized social or trade groups and are separated from the respectabilities of the middle-class suburb. It
would be wrong to say that Sargeson neglects the subtle dif-
ferentiations beween characters or the complex problems of
human relations, but he turns his back on the more sophisticated
areas in which people who have never been in touch with life

endlessly discuss and practise the intimacies of gracious living.
There is little in the situation of New Zealanders to provoke the
novel written under the influence of Henry James and his suc-
cessors, and little in the rather smug and philistine social life
to encourage the exploration of cultured sensitivity. "I've only
got a sort of polite interest in Jack's missis and those friends of
hers," the narrator of *The Hole that Jack Dug* comments.
"They're always talking about books and writers, but never any
I know anything about." [5] If only for this reason many readers
of the stories would strenuously deny that they are fully representative of New Zealand; and yet they provide an admirable
vantage point from which to view the buried and unrecognized
life not usually revealed in the gatherings of the all too articulate and the cosiness of the sheltered family circle. Sargeson
tends to see human nature in the raw, to uncover the concealed
but primary human affections and attitudes, to come closer to
Falstaff's "forked radish with a head fantastically carved." His
Teds and Bills and Toms and Freds are wandering and occasionally working in a world that seems to offer them no stable
foothold. They are "crouching down and holding on tight," as
the nameless small boy tries to indicate in *An Attempt at an
Explanation:*

If I'd been older perhaps I would have made a picture for myself of
the earth as just a speck of dirt drifting in space, with human
creatures crawling over it and crouching down and holding on tight
just as the lice had done on the back of my hand. [6]

The episodes that are described or dramatized in these stories
take place in a street, by a rubbish dump, in a public house in
Freeman's Bay or on a road up north, in a billiard saloon or
racing stable, on a woodpile by a shearing shed, in backyards
and boarding houses, on farms or on unfrequented parts of the
beach, and, rarely, in "the fag end part of a posh suburb." [7]
It is a lonely world, not because there are no people in the
neighbourhood, but because, as readers, we are caught up in
fragments of conversation and the instinctive responses of human
beings to an environment that is itself fragmented and is reflected in the episodes with which we are involved. It is lonely

because there is no connecting social thread, nothing that draws people together and unites them in a common aim, no acceptable values that give any meaning to life other than what can be derived from 'kindness in a corner' or in feelings of physical well-being. Sargeson's stories have their own 'figure in the carpet.' It is concerned with something not unlike the refrain that comes from the cracked gramophone in Virginia Woolf's *Between the Acts*, "Dispersed are we, who have come together," and led her to explore at a very different level "the wedge-shaped core of darkness" at the centre of the personality. The New Zealand writer, however, is more concerned with the simplicities of isolation, with the exercise of the elementary instincts for food, shelter, and affection and with the unexpressed perplexities of those whose aspirations may not be on a grand scale, but are nevertheless genuine and intensely human. They must crouch down and hold on tight, even when holding on tight brings little joy or satisfaction. They live in a solitude that is mental and spiritual, and all the more disturbing because their minds are incapable of discovering the source of their unhappiness. They are bewildered people, like the Dalmatian and the narrator in *The Making of a New Zealander,* who can find no escape from a world pain they can neither explore nor describe other than by a night of drinking lots of wine and getting "very, very drunk."

You too, Nick said. You think that you and me are born too soon? What do you think?
He said it over and over, and I couldn't look him in the face. It had too much of that sadness. . . . I mightn't have put it in the way Nick had, I mightn't have said I was born too soon, but Nick knew what he was talking about. Nick and I were sitting on the hillside and Nick was saying he was a New Zealander, but he knew he wasn't a New Zealander. And he knew he wasn't a Dalmatian any more.
He knew he wasn't anything any more.[8]

Again, Sargeson's people may be like Mr. Williams, the eccentric tomato grower in *A Man of Good Will* who had left his safe job in a big store because "it was wrong of people to shut themselves away from the sun and fresh air by working in such places, except that you went home at night it was just as though

you'd been put in gaol. As for people who worked inside cages
behind the counters of banks, or sat all day going up and down
in lifts—well, you might just as well live in a cage out at the
zoo." [9] He had set out to find a new way of living, but had
found it not as easy as he had thought. "You could count yourself one of the lucky ones if you got plenty to eat and a good
share of sunshine and fresh air, and didn't have to dress up to
go to work. The only thing that worried him, he said was that
he hardly ever had enough spare time to read a book. And the
joke of it was he'd thought when he started out he was going
to have plenty." [10]

Many of them are hurt people who scarcely recognize how
or why they have been hurt, like Mrs. Crawley in *An Affair of
the Heart,* who waited every night at the bus stop for her son
who never came, or like Miss Briggs, who sold pigs' trotters
and never smiled but passed down the street every day carrying
two heavy suitcases. They are tormented by emotional compli-
cations they cannot fully understand because the emotions are
'outsiders' like themselves.

Nevertheless, they all live in an authentic New Zealand world
which is brought to life not by intrusive descriptions but by the
seemingly casual detail and a surrounding atmosphere that is
almost an extension of their own characters. Formal description
would be out of place in stories that assume an environment in
order to explore human attitudes, and, wisely, Sargeson avoids
it. Even those of his later stories which abandon the first person
narrator never become discursive by forsaking the principle of
relevance; and the background is never described for its own
sake. An old woman may dig for *pipis* by the seashore, two
young men may row far out in the gulf to hunt for mussels on
submerged rocks, a youth may attempt to take a large wether
down through the bush and along a creek, seagulls may make
their "horrid squabbling noises" as an old man on the waterfront
tells about the strange and pathetic relationship between Bandy
and Myrtle, or a farmer may be turning up yellow clay as he
ploughs; but the author, who had himself been so affected by
the sights and sounds of the New Zealand bush and seascape,
remains content to evoke the spirit of place by details that
emerge from the situation and are never imposed upon it. His

success is such that most New Zealand readers find themselves in touch with a world that is indisputably New Zealand. Writing in the *New Zealand Monthly Review* Dennis McEldowney observed: "Sargeson's world stands clear as his own creation, a reflection of the world he wrote from, a comment on it, but not that world. His restraint and control, the precision of his ear and (something which has not been given the attention it deserves) of his eye, surprise anew."[11] This comment—"a reflection of the world he wrote from . . . but not that world"—should be emphasized, for the art of what I have called 'imaginative realism' should never be confused with 'realism.'

II   *The Moral Fable*

Most of Sargeson's characters in their settings are obscurely or vividly aware that something is radically wrong with the civilization of which they find themselves a part. A few of the earlier stories take the form of a brief moral fable or a simple parable; and because the truths enunciated smack of the preacher or social reformer they have been condemned as opinionated, even if amusing. This is to misunderstand the nature of the moral fable. Necessarily, it avoids subtlety, and the fragment of doctrine it contains is reinforced by a simple correspondence. The wooden leg and the knotty, close-grained body of Silas Wegg in *Our Mutual Friend* admirably indicate his hard and grasping character. Sargeson used such correspondence with telling effect. The "hard knocker" of the business man in *Conversation with my Uncle* becomes the objective correlative for the hard hearts and unimaginative minds of a whole segment of the human race. Of this prototype the nephew observes:

He can't suppose. So I said, say anyone went to a picnic they wouldn't try to monopolise the bananas, would they? Not if they were decent? He said, no, of course not. Then I asked him, what about the social picnic? Social picnic? He repeated the words. He didn't understand and I had to leave it at that. He was so puzzled I felt sorry for him.[12]

He concludes with the remark "Oh Lord! it's a good job everybody isn't like my uncle. We don't want a world full of dead men walking about in hard knockers."

In *A Piece of Yellow Soap* the narrator is the milkman, who repeatedly fails to collect the money owed by the woman who came to the door holding a piece of yellow soap. "The more I argued the tighter the woman would curl her fingers on to the soap; and her fingers, just out of the washtub, were always bloodless and shrunken. I knew what they must have felt like."[13] Within the space of forty-odd lines the piece of yellow soap becomes a symbol of hardship and human suffering and dumb protest, so that the conclusion makes its impact on the reader with far greater force and economy of language than a more elaborate and subtly developed story might produce. "Well, she is dead now, that woman. If she passed into Heaven I can't help wondering whether she passed in holding tight to a piece of yellow washing soap. I'm not sure that I believe in Heaven or God myself, but if God is a Person of Sensibility I don't doubt that when He looked at that piece of yellow washing soap He felt ashamed of Himself." More fully developed but scarcely any longer is such a small moral fable as *Cowpats*, in which the younger children on a farm used to get up early to do the milking and, because their boots were never watertight, preferred to patter across the paddocks with bare feet. One of them discovered how comforting it was to warm them in freshly dropped cowpats, but later the youthful narrator, having stayed in town with an uncle who owned a hotel, abandoned the practice. He had seen an old man who had asked the porter if he could warm his hands in a bucket of water. "At that age to see an old man who might be glad of a few cow-pats to warm himself up in was somehow a bit too much for me."[14]

Although there are many notable precedents which might seem to justify the attempt to write the brief moral fable, the prevailing literary climate is one that is unfavourable to it. Anything that gives the slightest indication that the reader is being 'got at,' that he is at the receiving end of a message, is regarded as damaging to artistic value. There is no necessity to defend Sargeson for those early attempts at a kind of writing which was partly encouraged by the depression period and partly by the leftwing periodical, *Tomorrow*, in which they were first published. Some of them are slighter even than their length would suggest, but none of them becomes strident or overassertive; and 'opinionated' is not a happy word with which to describe them or their author. They are humane and penetrating little parables that nearly always succeed in rendering an episode in an unexpected but significant manner. Nevertheless, Sargeson was experimenting; and as he gained confidence, clarified his aims and allowed his perceptions full play, he found, a little to his surprise, that the language structure was developing a quality that was at once individual and expressive. It was only then that he was able to achieve greater subtlety and to move away from the parable in order to probe deeper into the human condition and human attitudes.

Good Samaritan is an interesting example of the parable that without emphatic overtones explores a moral dilemma with finesse and complete control of language. The narrator's pal, Jones, rough, kindly, sensitive but more adequate in his response to a situation than in analyzing it or his own feelings, relates how on the previous evening he had crossed a rubbish dump and seen a man in dungarees lying doubled up and "retching something awful." What worried Jones was that he had done nothing except walk up and down and then go on his way. The conversation between the two friends constitutes the whole of the story; but its success is due to the contrast between the uneasy suspicion of Jones that he had done perhaps the right thing for the wrong reasons and the easy obtuseness of the narrator who advises him to dismiss the incident from his mind. The reader is himself forced to take part in the tiny drama because its meaning is found to lie at some distance from any of the three participants' points of view. The narrator's repeated "Forget it" becomes an ironic commentary underlining a dilemma that is far more complicated than a casual reading might suggest. What is involved is not only the validity of the original parable and its application in a modern world of policemen and drunken sailors and respectable citizens, but also the relation between motive and act, between theory and practice, between reason and instinct and between civilized behaviour and the dictates of the heart.

That sailor would have hated me if I'd interfered, wouldn't he've? Gosh, say I'd landed him in Court?

You'd certainly have been popular.

It's no good believing in Christianity now, is it?

Not if it doesn't fit in.

Well, it doesn't. I suppose he went back to his ship and skited about the time he'd had.

If he was drunk I suppose he did.

He was drunk. About an hour later I saw him down by the wharf. He was just a bit shaky.

You silly old man, I said. Forget it.

I can't. He might have passed out. I walked up and down and then I walked away.[15]

A more developed illustration of the ambiguities of a situation is to be found in *A Good Boy*. The boy who never wanted to be a good boy is trying to write the story of his life so that his little sister will know that he never wanted to be a good boy, and yet he has killed the girl with whom he was in love. In its oblique way and by the ambiguous use of the word 'good' from the standpoint of the boy, his parents, of his kindly and not altogether disreputable companions, from the standpoint of the reader and of conventional society, Sargeson is able to say more in this story about what is usually called juvenile delinquency, and also about conceptions of righteousness and self-righteousness, the deadened responses of the respectable conformers and the bewildered responses of the unregulated heart, than many a story or document ten times its length. It is a story that ironically underscores the habitual clichés about the moral behaviour of the unthinking. The irony is deeper and more subtle than Professor Horsman seems to think in his article on "The Art of Frank Sargeson."[16] It is directed not so much towards "a profounder corruption with which his parents had little to do" as towards a profounder bewilderment about moral values, a bewilderment that is to be detected both in the boy and in those that self-righteously condemn him, a bewilderment that, again ironically, is being transmitted to his little sister. *A Good Boy* demands from the reader intelligent cooperation in that he must attempt to distinguish between a crime that has been committed for the wrong reasons, the reasons that are found by unfeeling, conventional and unhappy people, and the behaviour of the humane but unregulated who, whatever their deficiencies in

understanding or social reputation, are not closed-in and inhibited. The story is concerned with a corruption that is by no
means only the boy's, but of a whole society which has lost its
way in a dark wood of repression and callousness.

In *A Man of Good Will*, first published in the Australian
Bulletin in 1941, Sargeson expands the small social parable that
had interested him into a more sustained and elaborate story in
which character, incident, description and angle of vision are
interwoven with skill and sardonic humour. Our view of David
Williams, the eccentric tomato grower, is a composite one. It
is presented by the narrator who as a boy worked for him and
as a man looks back with imperfect understanding of the motives
that led his former employer to his last grotesque, half-ridicu-
lous and half-heroic gesture of protest against the idiocies of
a money-crazed and destructive civilization. We see David's
eccentricities through the sympathetic but uncomprehending
mind of the boy and through the overheard opinions of parents
and neighbours; but the narrator is also able to evoke a picture
of the earthy paradise in which he worked, and of the theories
and actions of the tomato grower himself. With its description
of luxuriance, the scorching sun, the damp, manure-sodden
ground, the hot smells of growth and soil, the tomatoes in deep
layers in the packing shed, the story becomes a hymn of praise
to the fertility of earth and the creative labour of man. Prices
fall because of the abundance, but the tomatoes swell and ripen
without check. Instead of burying half his crop in a deep pit
as advised by the growers' association, David Williams with
infinite care builds by his front gate a monstrous pyramid of
ripe and polished tomatoes, a huge and glowing sepulchral
monument of living tomato flesh, erected not to the glory of
man but to his folly. At the same time this pyramid, so lovingly
wrought, becomes a memorial to man's creative ability, even if
decay lies at the centre as the tomatoes rot in the scorching
heat. "I'd helped him do the work," observes the narrator "and
just to stand and look at the result gave me a wonderful feeling
of being satisfied. Perhaps I'd never before understood what deep
feelings you could have over things you'd made happen under
your own hands. Perhaps I understood even more than that. I
may have understood that the feeling had nothing to do with

the money." [17] Another level of irony is still in reserve, however, for a sudden violent storm flattens the still-ripening crop and turns it into a tangle of twisted plants. Both man and boy throw themselves into the arduous task of restoring order; but after their efforts David continues to sit by his front gate and once again builds his vast pyramidal pile. A story that at its surface level remains one describing the eccentricities of a man of good will becomes both a hymn of praise and a commination against the sterility of a manmade economy that places greater value in destruction than on creation.

In *The Hole that Jack Dug*, published in *Speaking for Ourselves*, a collection of New Zealand short stories compiled by Frank Sargeson in 1945, a yawning hole replaces the monstrous pyramid of the earlier story in which it was a David who had paid his tribute to the God of fertility. The later story is concerned not with the House that Jack built but with the Hole that Jack dug. No one, least of all his wife, who wishes he would find a better job than working in a quarry, "meaning by a better job one that brings in more pay, without it mattering if its only senseless and stupid sort of work you have to do," [18] knows why this blue-eyed giant of a man is digging the hole close to the washhouse wall instead of getting on with the garden. His friend, the narrator, has sense enough to ask no questions, for Jack is "such a good-natured cuss, always wanting everything in the garden to be lovely for everybody that walks the earth" and he also had the habit of answering questions very indirectly. The labour, shovelling, the carting away of the rubble, the undercutting and propping that went into the digging of the hole fascinates the reader. The absurd but tragic meaning of it all begins to dawn, though it is never made explicit, as the aeroplanes drone overhead, and Jack, sitting on the edge of the huge pit, answers the complaints of his wife, "You see dear, Jack went on saying, though you could hardly hear him for the noise of the planes. You see dear, he said, we have more important things to do than those boys flying up there. Or at any rate, he went on, just as important." With the same incredible energy the hole is filled in again, and the only comment Jack made was that he must busy himself with the winter garden. A last wry twist is given to the fantastic anecdote when his friend tells us that only a little later Jack earned a considerable amount digging shelters for neighbours during the Japanese scare, but he made no attempt to dig one for his own family. This well-told story has the exuberance of a practical joke combined with the significance of a partially concealed parable; but the ironic interplay of character and scene gives it a quality that makes it memorable also for its craftsmanship.

It would encourage a wrong perspective towards Sargeson's work to lay too much stress either on the implicit or explicit criticism of the social wilderness in which his characters grope their way or on the harsher aspects of the world that emerges *from* rather than is described *in* them. He is no blatant propagandist or strident philosopher using the short story to achieve some extra-literary purpose. In his later stories he is an explorer of those qualities which, even in people who reject or have been rejected by civilized society and its packaged morality, are a guarantee that the common human aspirations are always valuable. These are the qualities that do more than hint at an inarticulate emotional life and a striving towards something that perhaps under more favourable conditions might lead to the beginnings of a richer and more satisfying existence. Sargeson had never forgotten the promise that the wild honeysuckle tree had held for him, nor his revulsion away from the withering of the instinctual life of which in those far off days he had become dimly aware. What he continued to seek for in his stories was something that contained within itself the seeds of a social sentimentalism frequently present when writers concern themselves with 'natural man' and his untutored emotions, when they react violently against what they regard as the false values of an over-sophisticated and artificial environment, and find themselves drawn towards some modern equivalent of the 'noble savage' heresy. E.M. Forster, who has himself emphasized the qualities represented by Stephen Wonham in *The Longest Journey*, has commented that Sargeson "believes in the unsmart, the unregulated and the affectionate" [19] and praises him because he does not force these qualities on our attention in such a way that we are led to wallow in a semi-articulate form of sentiment.

His characters, like his prose, are pruned down to the bare essentials, and rarely outgrow the spontaneous behaviour of the very young, although their appetites are those of adults. They look back, like Freddy Coleman in *An Affair of the Heart,* to their childhood on the beaches and farms of New Zealand, wistfully recalling the times when life was less complicated and more innocent, "Well, it's all a long time ago. It's hard now to understand why the things that we occupied our time over should have given us so much happiness. But they did. As I'll tell you, I was back in that bay not long ago, and for all that I'm well on in years I was innocent enough to think that to be there again would be to experience something of that same happiness." [20] The final comment of the narrator in that strange little story, *A Hen and Some Eggs,* is "Children are rather like hens. They know things that men and women don't know, but when they grow up they forget them." [21]

Since Sargeson began to write, but not necessarily owing to his influence, the innocent eye of childhood has become an ever-recurring motif in developing New Zealand literature, and points to a disillusive tendency not altogether unexpected in a young country that has failed to fulfil the promise that it seemed to hold for youthful idealists. Some of the most moving representations of human loneliness in Sargeson's stories are seen through the minds and emotions of children; but the loneliness is accompanied by a straining towards a simple conception of community and fellowship. It was the little boy in *An Attempt at an Explanation* who perceived the relationship between the silkworms and the lice and the worms and the blackbirds and himself; and a story that offers more than is sometimes supposed is the curiously titled *Tod.* As Bill Pearson has pointed out, the word "suggests *God,* and there is a striking affinity in theme and title with *Waiting for Godot.* But more than this, Tod is German for death." [22] The story itself is disarmingly simple. A little boy and his younger sister are playing by a fence, quarrelling and being affectionate by turns. Their awareness of each other's company, as they play intermittently with their kitten among the dandelions, is not sufficient to hide the ache of loneliness and aimlessness. Their bickering and the little boy's outbursts of unkindness and sympathy are merely indications of a void in their lives that at the moment nothing seems to fill. Again and again they stand by the fence and call "Tod," and after the boy has thumped his little sister and she has trotted inside to tell, he still stands by the fence singing out "Tod." "Everything would be just all right if only Tod would come on over. And he was far too young to know that he hadn't got the name exactly right." [23]

Stories such as these come alive not only because they contain fragments of experience from which wider areas of human life may be viewed, but because they are presented by means of vivid and recollected perceptions. In *An Attempt at an Explanation* the small boy records that "if I got tired of listening to the sermon I'd play with the tassels on the end of mother's fur, or she'd let me take her hand and I'd run my finger round the seams of her glove." [24] And in *Chaucerian* "The little girl had a rag doll under her arm, and after she had stood on her toes and tried to look over the bar she came out to the door and tried to make the rag doll sit on the door-knob." [25] In *Toothache* the story becomes one of 'I suffer, therefore I am': "He stared hard at the dark but he couldn't see anything. And there wasn't a sound. Yet he knew he was awake by the feel of the bed and his toothache. Granma, he said, Granma." [26] His grandmother picks the small child up and carries him to her bed, where she slides a finger into his mouth and rubs some powder on the hollow tooth. The brief story ends with the child asleep in his grandmother's arms, "But his granma didn't go to sleep. She was just a fat old woman with a few bits of hair hanging down, and she lay there, quite still, holding the boy in her arms. And all night she was staring hard at the dark." The ache of loneliness and suffering which begins and ends the fragment is relieved by the warmth of affection and consolation at its centre. With less control, with even a shade of added emphasis, a story such as this could readily turn into a magazine tear-jerker, but because Sargeson does not lose control, reduces his words to a minimum and makes no attempt at a commentary, it becomes more than a facile comment on the human scene.

III   *Loneliness and Fellowship*

A return to the innocent eye of childhood may sometimes be interpreted as an evasion of the treatment of adult tenderness

and affection. This is not true of Sargeson, although in much
New Zealand writing it is apparent that only rarely is there to
be found an adequate rendering of intimate human relations.
His characters may seem to be emotionally deprived but, because he has chosen to describe a world of the lonely and displaced, he is able to come closer to an inarticulate life that is
far more common than is usually imagined. As has been frequently noted by social observers, New Zealanders tend to be
laconic, off-hand, and perfunctory in the expression of strong
feelings; halting and shame-faced rather than stubbornly re-
served. Sargeson's people are not deprived of the instinct to
love, of the need for affection, of the hunger for fellowship;
but the world they inhabit, the moral climate in which they
live are not conducive to the cultivation of refined sentiments
or the development of adequate responses. Nevertheless, they
conceal beneath their crude and unpolished exteriors something
that is truer and more basic than can be gleaned from the
more voluble utterances of the supremely intelligent. They materialize as persons because they are made vocal by the narrator, the friend, listener, or observer, even if he shows himself
only partially aware of the significance of the story he tells. The
reader is made more perceptive because behind the people there
is always the author who, in spite of his detachment, is able by
the careful manipulation of structure and phrase to express more
than his characters understand.

Sargeson is rarely if ever concerned with what George Eliot
called "the twanging of the old Troubadour strings" [27] or with
what she describes, quoting King James, as a woman's "makdom
and her fairnesse." In their affections his characters hover on
the edge of a no man's land of emotional catastrophe that remains uncharted and unanalyzed. They hunger for some kind of
fufilment that is not identified even by themselves. The story
that gave his second volume its name, A Man and his Wife, is
a bizarre comedy with tragic overtones. There is no "crude and
sneering insistence on sexual abnormality," [28] as James K. Baxter
maintains, but an awareness of varieties of human tenderness
that, in spite of his refusal to commit himself to explicit state-
ments, frequently becomes a dominant note in his stories. Beneath the hard surface texture of his writing lies the deeper note

of pity for human beings caught within the entanglements of
emotions they do not comprehend, entanglements that indicate
the need for companionship, the intense desire to receive and
to give affection. *A Man and his Wife* is set during the slump,
but as the narrator, a relief worker, observes of that time of economic depression "it put a certain sort of comradeship into life
that you don't find now." [29] Ted Watts was also working on
relief and was separated from his wife, so the two friends lived
together in an old shed on the outskirts of the town; and Ted
brought his dog, the main cause of his separation from his wife.
The dog died; and Ted bought a canary on which he lavished
the same kind of attention that had made Mrs. Watts say "a
man ought to put his wife first." When the canary escapes during a wild party in the shed, Ted returns to his wife. "I said
he'd better try another dog, but he said no. I've still got the
wife, he said. The wife never let me down, he said. No, I said.
It was all I could think of to say." *A Man and his Wife* is an
absurdly pathetic story, and it is pathetic in terms of each of
the three characters because the channels of emotional communication are clogged. Separation is its main theme, and even
the narrator is left companionless: "Until the finish of the slump
I was living on my own, and occasionally I'd sort of wish that
Ted hadn't been so careless with his canary." Life serves separation orders on the motley array of characters in Sargeson's stories—"Dispersed are we; who have come together."

This sense of a disconnected world where the human beings
are separated by the inability to respond completely to the
secret urgings of the heart, by social barriers and by the lack
of relation between what is felt and what is accepted according
to the conventional moral standards of society's "insiders," is
powerfully expressed in story after story. Like Freddy Coleman
in *An Affair of the Heart*, Sargeson does not "set out to philos-
ophize"; but he is able to uncover the dumb strivings of human
beings and to create in the spiritual aridity of their environment
some oasis in which small grains of loving kindness, although
unable to thrive, can produce at least impressive if stunted
growth. It is not until Freddy Coleman is walking northwards
to a job on a fruit farm that he understands "how anything
in this world that was such a terrible thing could at the same

time be so beautiful." The "terrible thing" was not the tragic love of a man for a maid but the consuming love of a toothless old woman for her son, who never returned to the derelict shack by the beach where she lived. The effect of the story is a consequence as much of its structure as of the poignancy of the emotion which is, as usual, only obliquely described. The double angle of vision (the narrator young and grownup) and the careful control of the different periods of time from which the episode is viewed, together with the rendering of the sights and sounds of the beach scene, without recourse to florid description, show how effective bare and simple writing can be.

These qualities are even more apparent in the *Old Man's Story*, where the seagulls on the waterfront, a sordid court case read in a newspaper, and the thrice-uttered word "Terrible!" lead to the account of an episode that took place half a century or more previously, when the frail old man sitting on the bench was a boy of fourteen. It is the pathetic story of the strange attraction between a wiry little man in his fifties and a thirteen-year-old girl, a story that never came into the court and has little to do with sexual perversion or juvenile precociousness.

Bandy and Myrtle were sitting on the seat. Bandy was in his working clothes but Myrtle seemed to be in her nightgown, at any rate the boy could tell she had bare feet. And they were sitting there without saying a word, the old man said, sitting a little apart but holding each other's hands. Every now and then the girl would turn her face to Bandy and he'd lean over to kiss her; or Bandy would turn his face and she'd lean over to kiss him. That was all there was to see, the old man said. Nothing more than that. It amounted to this, that bad old Bandy had got the girl, this young Myrtle, with her silly curls, out on the seat with him, and there was nothing doing except those kisses. And the whole time the boy stood there watching he never heard them say a thing.

It was a tremendous experience for a boy, the old man said, too big for him to be at all clear about until later on in life. All he understood at the time was that he had somehow managed to get life all wrong. Like all boys he thought he'd got to know what was what, but as he stood there in the dark and watched Bandy and Myrtle he understood that he had a lot to learn. He'd been taken in, he thought. It wasn't a pleasant thought, the old man said.[30]

In other hands this story could have been disgusting or simply abnormal, but it is treated with a rare sympathy and with understanding; not by the boy, for it was all too much for him and he only knew "that he had a lot to learn." It was not learnt by the listener from the old man sitting by the waterfront, for his comments scarcely go beyond an observation on the sordid court case: "But people say, I said, what can you do?" and at the end of the story "I see, I said, and the old man got up to go." Nor was it learnt by the old man who told the story about Bandy and Myrtle, for he is recalling the strange experience he had witnessed when he was only a boy. The sympathy and understanding is generated by the setting, the ageless sea and the seagulls, the old farm house buried in honeysuckle and rambler roses where Bandy and Myrtle worked, by the way in which the interaction of time and place work on the emotions, above all, by what could be called the understanding "eye" which perceives that in human relations there is still a lot to be learnt; and, though judgement comes swiftly, the sympathetic imagination is even more important. How often is there more than a touch of beauty in what the moralists call evil? The question remains unanswered except by the sentence: "He understood he had a lot to learn."

Because he has always been drawn to the drifters, the forgotten men and women, to those who have not become submerged in domesticity or declined into the somnolence of the suburbs, Sargeson has chosen to explore some of the emotional experiences of "the unsmart, the unregulated and the affectionate." He has not been drawn to them for sentimental, social, or political reasons, but because he discovered early in his career that there was truth in the remark, quoted by Jones in *The Good Samaritan,* "a drunken sailor's nearer to God than a Presbyterian parson." [31] Beauty, affection, pathos, and tragedy reside in the dilapidated boarding house, are encountered in the back streets and on isolated farms and beaches as often as they are to be found in the homes of the cultivated; but in their loneliness, in their secret and inexpressible desires, the displaced and the established are not as far apart as is sometimes imagined.

When it is remembered that the experience of solitude and the intense longing for human warmth are not a monopoly of a nar-

row segment of humanity, Sargeson's stories can be seen in their
wider context. For his characters, fringe though they may be,
love can be a consuming, a bitter, a terrible emotion and should
not be identified with "the twanging of the old troubadour
strings," for it can manifest itself in a thousand different ways.
In a wisely excised passage in *Old Man's Story*, Sargeson had
referred to the incident of Bandy and Myrtle sitting on the seat
together as having "something that had a touch of beauty perhaps, though he never used the word beauty." [32] Yet, such a
word, although better omitted from the story, is exactly the
word that a critic may be permitted to use as he tries to convey
the notion that larger areas of life are illuminated than the re-
strictions imposed by artistic compression might seem to imply.
Such a slight episode as is contained in *Three Men* successfully
avoids the sentimentality of the usual magazine story. It escapes
insignificance because, although merely concerned with the longings of two lonely girls to be taken out in the evening by two
young men they had picked up at the races, it gives a gentle
and passing glance towards the unspoken memories of their
deaf old landlady, whose drunken husband had left her. It is
written in the form of a letter to a friend of one of the girls and
recounts the fiasco of their anticipated evening, otherwise containing little within it than the description of a day at the races
and of waiting for a telephone call that never came. However,
a true and genuine vein of feeling can be detected in the midst
of its vulgarity of expression and its naive sententiousness—"if
we can't be kind to each other what I say is we all ought to be
dead";[33] and we are left with old Mrs. Potter crying as she knits,
for the story is one of *Three Men* and not only of two rather
silly and flighty but lonely girls.

    That a satisfying mental and emotional relationship can exist
between a man and a woman is evidently not a theme which
particularly attracts Sargeson, although the ending to *Chaucerian*
should not be forgotten any more than the tough racehorse
trainer and his wife in *A Pair of Socks* and the surprise of the
narrator because the unemployed fitter in *Big Ben* "thought the
world of his missis," even though he could not express his feelings and neither of them talked overmuch. What does interest
him is that deep, instinctive groping towards relationship and

love which even among the deprived and alienated finds its outlet in a variety of tortuous and self-destructive ways. Early
sketches, as *In the Midst of Life, They Gave her a Rise,* and
In the Department, touch lightly on the frustrated existence of
those who have turned their backs on opportunity and have no
one to whom they can communicate their almost deadened love
of life. In the first of these brief vignettes the narrator's unmarried cousin, Frances, who feels she has had no life at all, bored
and soured by housekeeping for Uncle Joe, by unadventurous
respectability and ingrained prudishness, finds her real world in
the novels of Ethel M. Dell and in romances about Wagner
which, with a complete disregard for probability, she identifies
with contemporary New Zealand. In the midst of life we are in
death, and the narrator decides to give up going to see Uncle
Joe and Frances because "it's too much like a cemetery." The
explosion in the ammunition factory in *They Gave her a Rise*
thrusts Sally Bowman's mother into a paroxysm of hysterical
sobbing and self-accusation for having made her take a job
there; and the almost imperceptible changes in her recovery
when she finds her daughter is among the survivors are handled
admirably by the catholic narrator. Thus, it soon becomes evident that the need to make ends meet and the certainty of comparatively high wages have reduced her maternal warmth, and
her assurances to the God in whom she has no belief, to the
frigid and querulous demand that Sally should return when the
works open again. *In the Department* is set among the files in the
basement of a government building where Mr. Flyger, one of
"the old duds," has fallen in love with a very young girl, and
with a mixture of pathos and absurdity cries, "I've gone to her
people and they say no. My life is dry sand, and my heart has
withered up." [34]
With ascending degrees of success, each of these stories is
stamped with the characteristic signature of the author; but as
accords with its increased length and the later date, *The Colonel's Daughter,* published in *Landfall* in 1955, has qualities that
are more varied and subtle. Although Sargeson here abandons
the semi-articulate characters which had provided themes for
the main bulk of his shorter experiments, he is able to orches-
trate his story by close attention to the past as well as to the

present, and the evocation of a local scene resembling that of
his boyhood. The white-haired and prim old lady, Miss Smith,
whom the narrator meets in a little tourist hotel, had been regarded as eccentric and immoral by a small-town community in
the Waikato. At dinner and on the verandah, drinking coffee
while they wait for the moon to rise ("one can be sure it won't
miss an appointment even though it may turn up late," [35] the old
lady observes), she recalls with some enjoyment the scandalous
little episode that led to her sudden retirement to the conti-
nent. It is a tale that becomes the closest of any by Sargeson
to the eternal triangle of sex, but is told in his own characteristic
manner. It is of the "fallen woman," Daisy Willoughby, of small-
town nonconformist pressure to make her a human sacrifice at
the altar and of how her musical husband was enticed away by
the attractions of a grand piano and its mistress. Its theme is the
not unusual one of two young women who hunger for life and
not for the death of the spirit, of a talented but weak young man
who seeks for something that cannot be obtained in his circum-
scribed environment. Each of the characters misses an appointment with a more fortunate fate and slides into a regretful old
age, with the wasted talents of spirited youth but a faded memory. The achievement in the story, however, is not dependent on
the slightly bizarre variation in the shape of the triangle, not
even on the way in which it recaptures in its small compass the
atmosphere of a restricted and hidebound society with its social
divisions, its gossip, its respectability and moral imperatives, but
on the careful precision of language used by the dry and still
eccentric Colonel's daughter, one of the Porterhouse-Smiths.
Her assumption of social and intellectual superiority, her mock-
ing air and her barbed comments on "the proper environment
of the proper people," her reticences, her disarming frankness,
and her prim but slightly pathetic determination to keep her appointment with the moon are not merely written on the printed
page. Her language is a language that can be heard. Sargeson
writes with many voices, and even the voices of his useful nar-
rators are never quite the same.

Nothing could offer a greater contrast to the liveliness of the
caustic little spinster's conversation than that of the smooth,
self-righteous and canny Robert Wilson in *The Undertaker's*

Story, first published in 1954. This time the setting is not one of a tourist hotel but of a seaside public house on the edge of a harbour. The author as narrator takes little part in the small drama that is unfolded in his presence, but by his uncustomary perceptiveness he is able to establish both the scene and the contrast in character and fortune that becomes the subject of the story to which he listens. Sitting with his beer on the verandah, he has behind him the muffled roar of human voices in the stifling bar, and before him the fresh coastal breeze, the brilliance of the sun, and the high tide rolling on to the beach. His solitude is interrupted by the sound of a quarrel inside, immediately followed by the ejection of a thick stodgy figure summarily thrown on the sand. Soon afterwards he is joined by a natty little man who emerges from the bar and sits beside the crumpled bundle of clothes; and before the solitary watcher on the verandah is enacted a scene that provides an implied commentary on the story soon to be related:

When they at last stood up and parted, it seemed that the drunk was perhaps not so drunk. Quite steady on his feet, he returned from along the beach for the ceremony of trust and friendship. Hands were gripped and held, placed on shoulders and left there. It was a sort of tableau, or they might have been figures on a frieze. Beyond them the sea's dark blue suggested melancholy, and the unceasing movement seemed not to hold out any promise of permanency for their bond, but at least they stood on sand that was solid and clean after the high tide, and there was the sunlight for an impartial golden blessing.[36]

Even such a passage as this indicates that Sargeson has been prepared, in his later work, to adapt the stark manner of his early writing to the needs of more subtle situations, and yet, as *The Undertaker's Story* reveals, not to abandon his treatment of the buried and sensitive life of those who cannot wear their hearts on their sleeves. A partial explanation of the tableau that had been presented with a backdrop of the blue and restless sea is given by the local undertaker when he returns from his friendly mission; but the story that he tells is as much the story of a man who could not forgive himself for his failure as it is one of the self-satisfied Robert Wilson who was unaware that he needed to be able to forgive himself for his success. The two Scotsmen, Wilson and Duncan, one a lowlander and the other a highlander, had come out to New Zealand to find a place where they would not be pushed around, and both had been unsuccessful at the outset. Although Wilson was older and had come out first, their fortunes had been roughly parallel in marriage and employment; but the more astute and loquacious lowlander had later prospered as an undertaker and property owner, and Duncan, blundering and silent, with a taciturn wife and a small son, had found himself under obligations to his older acquaintance. His tragedy had been one of too strict a devotion to what he thought was his duty and too keen a sense of what he owed to his fellow countryman. The tragedy of Wilson, unacknowledged even to himself, was one of a spiritual deadness beneath a surface manner of kindliness and concern, while watching carefully how he could benefit from any situation. Sargeson's stories consistently peer through the appearance of things to their underlying reality; and some of his more impressive effects are gained when his characters betray themselves by their innocent remarks or abrupt monosyllables and uncover their raw and quivering nerves or their deadened sensitivity. As the dour and uncommunicative Duncan buries his child in a rude coffin, made by himself to avoid more obligations to the undertaker, he murmurs "Jock! my Jock." As the story concludes the intelligent listener asks Wilson, "did you ever marry again?"

Ay, he replied. I married my housekeeper. It was in keeping with my position when I was appointed a Justice of the Peace. My wife is a fine figure of a woman.

There was an indefinable something about his eyes—what is called a twinkle, I suppose.

And she has an excellent hand for cooking.

Yes, I said as I raised my hand for a goodbye. I'd expect that.[37]

The surface has cracked for a moment, and the reader knows that the imperturbable Wilson has not been as correct in his behaviour as he had expected Duncan to be; but he had always been prepared to make his bow to appearances.

If stories such as these are directed towards the exploration
of the different forms taken by human tenderness and the distor-
tions to which it is subject as social pressures manifest themselves, there are others in which pathos and tragedy enter
through the thwarting or suppression of powerful instincts. Because he deals with those who live on the outer borders of organized society, and therefore, more frequently than not, are
solitary and torn inwardly by conflicting passions, Sargeson is
led to areas of experience which may be more irregular and destructive. One of the earliest of the stories which tax the reader's
sympathy but enlarge his understanding is *I've Lost my Pal*, first
published in *Conversation with my Uncle and Other Sketches*
in 1936. The central character, George, is a sheep shearer who
sees no sense in a settled job. Each evening, after the day's work
is over, he dresses himself carefully and comes to sit with two
young companions, Tom and the narrator, on a woodpile near
which a chained dog barks incessantly. George files his nails,
combs his hair and talks about life and himself. According to
his own account he had no mother; as a young boy he had
been a Sunday School teacher's pet; he had no interest in women;
and every now and then "he sort of got tired inside. It was when
he sort of felt everybody he met was too silly to talk to, wouldn't
understand him if he did talk." [38] Summer evenings, the full
moon, the woodpile, the nearby shearing shed and the barking
dog provide the setting for a series of gruesome incidents of
cruelty and violence. No attempt is made to inspire horror or
sympathy. The style is simple, colloquial, and flat; and the only
comment that suggests any kind of emotion on the part of the
narrator is "I'm sore at losing Tom. I am that. But I have to
admit that he'd sometimes get on your nerves and make you feel
tired by arguing silly. Haven't you ever felt like that with anyone? Own up. I bet you have." [39] After such an ending and despite the criminal brutality of the actions related, it is not easy
to cast the first stone at the maimed character, George.

A Pair of Socks is a lighter sketch of two undersized stable
boys and a racehorse trainer and his wife, with overtones of
homosexual jealousy in an adolescent who is scarcely aware of
the nature of his impulses. In *Sale Day*, however, the isolated
farm, the kitchen fire and frying chops, the girl, the man, and

the randy tomcat provide the materials for a powerful conversational piece concerned with self-loathing and disgust. The brutal burning of the cat and Victor's remark, "Look here, Elsie . . . it's a fortnight to next sale day. If I was in your shoes I'd look round for another job," [40] brings to a horrifying climax the conflict suggested in such brief sentences as "Nature's bloody awful" and "I don't particularly like myself . . . any more than I like that cat." As Elsie says, the tom's behaviour may be only nature, but for Victor that is exactly the point. He is tormented by pride in his masculine virility, by his uncertainty whether he is able to control his sexual desires and by a violent revulsion against the knowledge of his own kinship with the animals, all of which find their outlet in the cremation of the live cat.

Sargeson's comparatively slender output is indicative of a refusal to write stories merely for the sake of dramatic narrative and of a desire to explore the varied responses of human beings to the experience of living. A Great Day, one of the longest of the earlier sketches, is more elaborately developed and sustained; and, partly because it is written in the third person, the attempt to evoke the atmosphere of the harbour and the Rangitoto channel has been successfully achieved. However, there are no slabs of description; and gulls, sun, wind, water, and tide, the mussels on the submerged reef, the rocking and direction of the dinghy with its ill-assorted pair as it moves into what seems a timeless world, all enter imperceptibly into the consciousness of the reader until his senses are tingling and identified with the seascape. It is a story the full impact of which comes only with the second reading, for it is only then on the long pull out to the reef that the conversation, guided by Fred, who lives on sustenance and from the fish he can catch in the harbour, turns into something like an ironic interior monologue of self-justification for the crime he is preparing to commit. This violent but evocative tale with its unpleasant ending is redeemed by the glimpses that are caught of a twisted mind in a weedy body, by a realization that if the blood of one so conscious of failure and physical inferiority has turned to gall, there still remains sufficient sensibility to make his life a misery as he starts on his solitary long pull back to the shore.

IV *The Later Stories*

The year 1945 marked a pause, a terminal point, in the experiments Sargeson was making with short stories. In the Collected edition (1964) all but three of those included, *The Undertaker's Story, The Colonel's Daughter,* and *A Personal Memory,* which belonged to the fifties, had been written before this date. He had become more and more preoccupied with other kinds of writing, in particular, with novels and plays. Nevertheless, in 1964 and 1965 appeared *Just Trespassing, Thanks, City and Suburban,* and *Beau.* Even in 1945 it was clear that Sargeson was not wholly dependent on the period of the Great Depression for material from which to create his characteristic sketches. *Last Adventure,* although mainly concerned with the impact made by a sudden realization of death on a young boy dreaming of a life of adventure, gave signs, like *The Hole that Jack Dug,* that within his range were more sophisticated levels of human life than those to which his roustabouts and solitary men and women were accustomed. As the Depression days receded and the welfare state came into existence he was much aware that the way he had chosen and the vision he had cherished of the New Zealand that could be were incompatible with the kind of economic earthly paradise that the Labour Party was busy ushering in, and that the likely result of its endeavours would be a society in which spiritual apathy would accompany the pursuit of Money, Time, and Success. In an article written in 1938 he defined an earthly paradise as "one that throws over hours for days, i.e., clocks for the sun," and he continued:

Mr. Savage's Paradise doesn't, I'm afraid, promise us anything as idyllically happy-go-lucky and free from the curse of hours as that. With so many hours on and so many hours off, the countryman of the future will live the life that the civil servant lives today. And what sort of a life is that? Well, I was one once and it was a life of hours. Every day, whether you felt in the mood for it or not, you had to sign on and sign off at certain times (though as it was before Mr. Savage took charge of us all, the time when you signed off was by no means as certain as the time when you signed on). . . . Instead of controlling and shaping your work according to your particular

nature you had to allow yourself to be controlled and shaped by
your work. It wasn't so much your work, however, that was the
burden. It was the Clock. Only by making a sort of superhuman
effort at your work could you keep the clock moving, over the last
hour particularly. The important question is how much satisfaction
can anyone who is not just a stick get from work of the kind that is
governed by hours? There is the Money of course, and the substitute
for Money in the future will be Security.[41]

Nearly thirty years later in his recently published *City and Suburban* the narrator says:

I have aimed at establishing myself as a man who can appreciate that
some very attractive flowers grow on what used to be a kind of dung
heap, sometimes called by fanciful names (such as Leviathan); but
which is nowadays more aptly described as a combined junk and
gadget heap, praised-and-damned as the welfare state—or sometimes
just praised as the affluent society. What are the advantages I derive
from that appreciation? Has the higher education sold me an outsize
pup or not? Answers to these questions wouldn't be just for me—as an
accountant I would say that to reckon accurately the number involved
could be a pretty sizeable job of computing, one requiring to be served
by the latest model electronic machine if the population explosion
and all such kindred phenomena are to be taken into account.[42]

As is immediately perceived both from the language and the
ideas of an extract such as this, Sargeson has developed a different voice, a voice that is closer to his own, one that had
been heard much earlier in *Letter to a Friend*, where he was
able to write easily and in harmony with the context:

Somehow the plane had killed my interest in his theorising. It was
brutal of me no doubt, but I said that immediate things had always
interested me most. And I quoted Blake, 'Turn away no more; why
wilt thou turn away? the starry floor . . .' But, I went on to say, that
up in the sky was the sort of immediate thing you were faced with
these days, and you just couldn't turn away.[43]

In *Just Trespassing, Thanks,* the young man with a rag of a
shirt and stove-pipe trousers of fancy material hauls from his
hip pocket a tattered copy of Matthew Arnold's poetry and pro-

ceeds to quote passages for the delectation of his unwilling and elderly host, whose attention is occupied by a Latin grammar; and Beau Ughtrey with his "superior pommy bastard" [44] accent can remember somewhat wistfully a novel by Thomas Hardy. Each of these stories, like those of the fifties, is no longer related even distantly to the moral fable which had interested him for a considerable time; and the slightly wry sense of humour which had sometimes characterized his early sketches is given fuller play.

The Last War, written by Sargeson in the thirties, had been a rather undistinguished attempt to see the world through the eyes of a schoolboy to whom the armistice had meant no more than a disruption of the annual sports day. The blood and tears of suffering had been represented by the return to the district of a legless man who was promptly invited to tea, but had nothing to say. The patriotic fervour meant a secret fear, towards the end of the war, that the boy's father might write on an unofficial form that he was unwilling to go and thus reveal his fear. It also meant that the farming uncles gave money and land to the patriotic fund and were able to retire a few years later. *City and Suburban* is a much more mature and complex account of what life means to a thirty-year-old man who was too young to go to the Second World War, who was allowed "to dig for victory" in the vegetable plot, and who missed his opportunity to become junior partner to his older brother on a milk-round. He was therefore "the end product of what may happen if you raise the school leaving age." [45] Already he is being affected by the rapid passage of the seasons and looks forward with undisguised foreboding to the time when he will find it difficult to fill in "the empty space between the morning and afternoon papers." Even his virility is sadly impaired by the lack of meaning that he suspects in a life that commutes between city and suburban; but the story is not primarily about the grim and symbolic trophy discovered on the beach by his children, nor about his unsatisfactory and perfunctory marital relations. It is a story that very competently succeeds in expressing those quintessential qualities that have accompanied the development of the welfare state, and, rather unkindly, are revealed in terms of his wife's attitudes. For her, an annual holiday consists of "golden days of

sun and games but with the lid taken right off," and the beatific
vision has turned into a vision of the here and now, where no
one grows older "(I mean beyond maturity), and could always
reckon on a large credit account at the Bank," where everyone
assumes that the right to happiness is inalienable and happiness
has reference to the precise here and now.

Two of the questions which, according to Sargeson, he has
been repeatedly asked are 'Why don't you write about decent
people?' and 'Why don't you leave off living as though the slump
is still on?' These may be pertinent questions for those who
did not have first-hand experience of relief work and queuing
up for sustenance or who had a belief, however weak, in the
doctrine of success and what William Morris called "useless
labour." Nevertheless, as a comment even on the sketches that
were to a great degree based on the hardships and injustices of
the depression, they completely miss the point, for his stories
centre mainly on the predicament of man at any time, in any
place, but with particular and precise reference to New Zealand. As the affluent society expanded with all its unwelcome
accretions his attitude did not change to any marked extent. If
such a word can be used in relation even to the weakest of his
moral fables, the 'strident' note detected by some of his critics
has softened. His tone has become more varied and the inflections of his voice more mellow. He can more easily combine
light-hearted or mordant humour with pathos and mingle a humane appreciation of life with a devastating criticism of its
social absurdities and failures.

Beau, which was published in *Mate* in 1965 and is not one of
the best of his stories, is mainly a character study of an elderly
man who from the time he was declared redundant in the thirties
had experienced unlimited and also "unfinancial" leisure. His
personal eccentricity, which developed when he discovered that
his rare conversations with the postman could be made more
frequent by writing letters to himself, is interwoven with what
amounts to a brief record of some important New Zealand attitudes from the depression times to the war years and afterwards. As an educated man with the right accent he was regarded as "unfortunate" because he was among the unemployed,
but during the war he graduated to a position of near popularity

in the voluntary organizations as "a showcase Englishman and part of the show put on for Americans." His later decline, after his miserable shack had been demolished to make room for the houses of war heroes, is treated with the sympathy and understanding of an author to whom the harmless follies of men are infinitely preferable to the impersonal mechanization of an industrial society.

A far more substantial story published in *Landfall* in 1964— *Just Trespassing, Thanks*—endeavours to portray the modern variety of the offbeat generation, living like Sargeson's earlier wanderers on the outer limits of society. The "suburban recluse," Edward Corrie, middle-aged and devoted for the time being to Latin syntax, is disturbed to find that three impossible young people, two boys and a girl, have been so inconsiderate as to sleep on the verandah in his stretcher bed. This discovery leads to an hilarious account of their unorthodox behaviour, from eating out of innumerable tins to quoting their own poetry and finally disappearing, motorcycle and all, into the suburban distance. It is one of Sargeson's most successful stories because it combines understanding with humour, revelation of character with social penetration, the individual with the type. Sargeson is still capable of examining the world that surrounds him with a keenly observant and comprehending eye. The ending gives some indication of the urbane and satisfying qualities of *Just Trespassing, Thanks*:

The young people were waving him goodbye as they crowded at the doorway. They were leaving him what remained of the tinned food, they said. Edward felt in his pocket and they declared, No, no, Mr. Corrie, you have them. They were gone, and he recollected that unless he was greatly mistaken they already had his loose change. He discovered himself to be exhausted and profoundly satisfied, a satisfaction which he had previously experienced only after carnal union on very rare occasions. To look out the window and discover the tiled roofs were still there was a surprise. Sylvarum numina. Perhaps the day had arrived for Ovid to be rewritten. It was not difficult to understand that deities would expect to be paid token money; but they on their part could hardly be expected to pay their regards to worldly morality.[46]

Throughout his career as a short story writer (though the word 'career' seems singularly inappropriate when applied to Sargeson), throughout his consistent dedication to the craft of fiction, he has shown his adherence to, if not always his achievement of, high standards of perfection. If good writing can be defined as the giving of the right emphasis in the right places, then he has demonstrated both in structure and content, identical as these may be, that he has been able to communicate an artistic vision that is without parallel in New Zealand letters. At the present time, with his work still unfinished and with competent writers still emerging, it would be not only difficult but futile to attempt to evaluate his work in terms of its permanent worth, more difficult and equally futile to measure him beside world writers with very different problems and different traditions. Nevertheless, for a long time it will be possible to maintain that his contribution to the art of the short story has been invaluable, stimulating, and impressive. He has created a coherent world composed of his private artistic vision, which has been founded on personal experience, on intense awareness of many aspects of New Zealand life and on the uneasy situation of twentieth-century man facing his own solitude. He has helped to mould the attitudes of many readers and also of many writers. He has become a part of New Zealand's developing tradition.

CHAPTER 4

The Unregulated Heart

"A man wants a mate that won't let him down."

I *Picaresque Novelette*

SARGESON's complete disregard for the normal requirements of well-defined literary categories has been disconcerting to readers and critics, and a source of irritation to publishers. As his intentions clarified and he was able to exert greater control over language and structure, he found himself forced to adapt and even to create forms that would give proper emphasis to his imaginative vision of life. Short stories as varied as *Good Samaritan, A Great Day,* and *The Undertaker's Story* provide a challenge to those who have accustomed themselves to the standardized tools of criticism and are unable to achieve the necessary flexibility which can accept them on their own terms. When *That Summer* appeared in three consecutive numbers of John Lehmann's *New Writing* it was difficult to know whether it should be approached as a short novel or as a long short story. Although its publication in the volume *That Summer and Other Stories* and again in the *Collected Stories* seemed to suggest that, apart from its length, it was in no way different from *Conversation with my Uncle* or *An Affair of the Heart,* there seemed no valid reason why it should be thus distinguished from the later *I for One* which, when it was printed in *Landfall* and as a separate publication, was described as a "short novel."

The difference between a long short story and a novelette may be of academic interest only. What is of greater import is the way in which *That Summer* approximates the picaresque, but cannot be completely identified with that form nearly so well as the much later *Memoirs of a Peon.* Professor Chapman once described it as "episodic, a clothes line of incident certainly, but after a peculiar fashion where the varying contexts have odd relations more powerful than the characters they contain." [1] It is almost inevitable that words like 'peculiar' and 'odd' will tend to crop up in connection with Sargeson's writing not because such epithets are particularly applicable but because it falls into a shape that is related to the pattern in life that "his idiosyncracy leads him to observe," and that pattern emerges from the world he sees and not from the conventions of literary art.

That Summer has a picaresque quality because by those who blandly accept the conventions and morality of a middle-class suburb its central character could be regarded as a shiftless rogue and an unprincipled adventurer, capable of using his wits in a number of disreputable ways to achieve a precarious financial stability. The account he gives of what was intended to be a summer vacation, spent in an unnamed city after he had turned in his job as a farm labourer, is composed of a series of loosely related and unspectacular episodes which provide material for the exploration of human attitudes rather than for the excitement of intrigue and unusual event. Bill, the itinerant worker with "itchy feet," is not a picaroon in the sense that his deeds are all-important and his ability to extricate himself from awkward situations is remarkable. He is not a mere peg on which the story is hung. He, himself, is the story; and his relations with other human beings, in particular Terry O'Connor, the consumptive barman, create both the interest and the significance of this deeply moving and powerful piece of fiction.

Bill, farm labourer and kitchen hand, possesses two qualities, either of which should be regarded as a necessary concomitant to the other—he can work and he can loaf. He can invite what others might call the 'soul,' although Bill has no soul of any measurable size to invite. He has affections and an interest in immediate objects, but no interior life or mental activity beyond a few banal reflections. He drifts through the summer days by the simple process of wandering about the streets, lazing on the beach in the hot sun or staying in bed half the morning with a *True Story* beside him. He has no home and no family ties. His attitudes may best be described by a series of negatives, for he has no religion, no politics, no morals, no desire to become part of a community or social group, no interest in getting on in the world, no attachment to money, possessions, or prestige of any kind. He is outside society and is wholly lacking in any wish to be on the inside. His happiness is very largely a matter of physical well-being, of a capacity to find pleasure in a few drinks at a pub, in yarning with a Dalmatian, in patting a stray dog, in picking up a sheila, in going to the flicks or in having a good counter lunch. His philosophy of life is contained in a few fragmentary injunctions to himself—"it's never much good wishing for things to be any different," "my idea of the johns is that a man wants to keep away from them no matter what goes wrong," "it doesn't matter what sort of a night you have, things are always different in the morning," "everybody must be pretty much the same in most ways if you could only find out."

It might be thought that a human being incapable of any but the most rudimentary responses to the experience of living, and with an intelligence level scarcely superior to that of a boy of twelve, could not offer a satisfactory centre of interest even to a novelette concerned with dingy boarding houses, back-street loafers and sordid restaurants and bars, particularly when it is Bill himself who is the narrator. Nevertheless Sargeson's uncanny knack of catching the inflections of the voice, of conveying mood and meaning through a limited vocabulary, of revealing half-expressed thoughts by the movement of language is everywhere apparent:

. . . being all on my pat up there that evening somehow gave me the dingbats properly. I couldn't decide what to do to fill in the time, and I couldn't keep my mind off thinking about a job. I tried reading my *True Story* but it was no good. I'd just lie on my bed but that was no good either, and I'd have to keep getting up to walk up and down. I'd stop in the middle of the floor to roll a cigarette and listen to them downstairs. I'd think, my God I've got to have someone to talk to, but even after I'd turned out the light and had my hand on the doorknob I'd go back and just flop on the bed. But the last time I flopped I must have dozed off, because I woke up lying in my clothes, and I wondered where the hell I was. I'd been dreaming, and I still seemed to be in the dream, because there wasn't one sound I could hear no matter how hard I listened. Then somebody started coughing and I knew where I was, but next minute I was back in the dream again, and I kept on dreaming and waking up right until it began to get light, though the last time I dropped off I slept a long time and never dreamt a thing.[2]

Bill is rough but kindly, crude but sensitive, self-sufficient but frequently lonely and aware of his solitude. He has a sociable disposition in the sense that he easily picks up casual acquaintances wherever he goes, in lodging house and on the street corner, in a public bar, at the police station, in tram or cafe kitchen; but with his longing to lavish affection on someone, he is always looking for a "joker who'd go solid with a cobber" because "a man wants a mate that won't let him down." It was different when he was working in the country: "Sunday afternoons on the farm when there was nothing else doing I'd go and shoot pigeons away up in the bush, and I wouldn't feel as much on my own as I did now in a town full of houses and people." [3] His sexual impulses remain at the level of a simple physical urge and his transient involvements with sheilas is of small account when compared with his desire to "go solid with a cobber" who might soften the ache of solitude, provide an object for his care and attention, and an outlet for his affectionate nature. As J. K. Baxter has observed, *"That Summer* is a love story," [4] but the love that it reveals and illuminates rather than describes is as far removed from the usual variations of the boy-meets-girl theme as it is from the homosexual innuendoes and explicit dramatizations that have become more and more familiar to readers. Indeed, the homosexual under-plot in *That Summer* serves an important function in that it helps to clarify the relationship between the rangy Bill and the ex-bartender, Terry, with his wrinkled Aussie face and hacking cough.

The difficulties of writing such a "love story" as this in the first person should not be underestimated. It is required of the author that he should be able to steer his course between the Scylla of a hard and rocky toughness and the Charybdis of an oozy sentimentality in such a manner that Bill, the narrator, is able to disclose his true feelings and qualities without the aid of intrusive explanation or analysis, and without departing from his characteristic mode of utterance. This, Sargeson triumphantly achieves. Although Bill is a sneak thief when necessary, a frequenter of bars and race courses, a picker-up of unconsidered trifles like Autolycus, although he finds himself in a prison cell for interfering with one whom he had mistaken for a woman, although he can think up ingenious schemes to defraud others and keep a roof over Terry's head and food for them both, he is so clearly one of "nature's gentlemen" that the reader becomes suspicious that a kind of personal sentimentality, apparently avoided, may be converted into a more serious and dangerous social sentimentality that has many parallels in the cult of the primitive. Bill is a generous, kind-hearted and sympathetic picaroon who, despite his toughness, is apologetic for and slightly ashamed of his natural instinct to help others at the expense of himself. He is ready to find excuses for the self-interest and calculating astuteness of those who impose on him or relieve him of his "few chips," and is quick to reject any suggestion of altruism in his own behaviour:

I went off whistling and feeling life was good when a man had a cobber like Terry to kick around with, and maybe I was feeling good because I was thinking what a hell of a good joker I was. Though if I was I was kidding myself, because when all is said and done I was only doing what I was to please myself, though it might have been a roundabout way of doing it.[5]

Except for the "demons," the official preservers of law and order, from whom he keeps away as far as he can, everyone is disposed to think well of Bill, both those whom he is easily persuaded to help with the price of a feed or a beer and those who can recognize that his good nature can be useful to them. His own astuteness extends little further than to the ability to think up on the spur of the moment some ingenious little plan whereby his present necessities, particularly where Terry is concerned, may be temporarily satisfied; and his frank and innocent enjoyment of well-being when he is in no immediate danger of having to go without a meal is as disarming as it is infectious. Even when he is looking for a job at the Registry Offices and is completely broke he can say, as he sits and dangles his legs over the side of the wharf with Terry, "I thought no man whose belly was full could have said it wasn't good to be alive. I wondered if Terry was thinking the same way, but a man never does ask those sort of questions, so instead I asked him if he'd have a smoke, and he made one but it made him cough." [6]

II *The Waif as Narrator*

Compared with any of Sargeson's early short stories *That Summer* has a far more complicated structure that belies its apparently picaresque form. It is one that is closely related to the direction imposed by the simple plot and, therefore, to the intentions of the author and the requirements of what he has to communicate by his selection of material. It is not merely a disconnected series of fragments, a "succession of accidents and sad misfortunes." Although seemingly fortuitous the earlier episodes are cunningly linked and are so constituted that they enable the author to disclose by slow stages the identity of Bill as a lovable human character in his own right and as one through whom the underlying theme may be conveyed.

The story begins with Bill, urged on by his innate restlessness to abandon his secure job and home on an isolated farm, preparing to walk the six miles to the nearest railway station. The farmer's wife had come out to say goodbye and given him a sovereign from a little bag which he had not seen before:

When I got down the road she came running along and grabbed hold of me for a kiss, and then she stood in the road and waved. She looked a bit of a sketch I can tell you, with her hair hanging down and her old man's coat on over her nightgown. I felt a bit sorry and wished in a way I wasn't going, because the farm away back there in the valley looked sort of nice and peaceful with the sun just getting up on such a fine morning, and only a sheep calling out now and then. . . .[7]

In town, after a walk round the streets and a feed while he wondered if he might pick up a girl, he finds himself at the Cleggs' lodging house, sandwiched in between a butcher's shop and a brick warehouse, and before long he is playing with the skinny-legged little girl, Fanny, underneath what they both call the money tree. It is here that Bill loses not the intended sixpence which Fanny was to find, but the golden sovereign which had been given him by the farmer's wife.

There is a faint element of the traditional fairy story or folk tale in Bill's small adventures. He is the good-hearted, carefree innocent whose deeds, however foolish and improvident in the worldly sense, always redound to his credit. His friendship with Fanny leads to his awareness of the presence in the same house of Maggie who will later be responsible for landing him in gaol; and Fanny's skinny legs are the theme on which her father, a former ship's cook, elaborates on the way to the pub where Bill first meets Terry O'Connor, the barman, who had formerly some connection with a racing stable. It is the political conversation between Mr. Clegg and another ship's cook, together with their fiery denunciation of "the system," which result in Terry's dismissal, and Terry himself proves to be another lodger in the Clegg establishment. Bill's wanderings round the streets and in the parks bring him into touch with a number of bums, drifters and unemployed with whom he strikes up temporary acquaintanceships which never ripen into the kind of companionship for which he longs. He meets Sam who cadges from him a meal, cigarettes, drinks, a visit to the flicks and to a dance where they are both kicked out. He talks with a Dalmatian family in an eating house, where later, in order to keep Terry, he will find a short-lived job in a kitchen. On the beach he meets Ted, who has no difficulty in relieving him of the remains of the money he had earned at the farm; and the next time he meets him will be while waiting to go into court to face a criminal charge.

All these episodes and many others are not only functional in the development of the plot and the building up of character, but combine to give a vivid picture of the kind of world in which Bill moves and has his being. The scenes in the Cleggs' boarding house with Maggie, whom the little girl, Fanny, refers to as Mrs. Popeye, because she is supposed to be the wife of a sailorman, the street and beach scenes, the description of the Dalmatian's kitchen, and the prison scenes are a constant reminder that Sargeson is skilful in rendering atmosphere and the spirit of place, whether the area described is sordid and unsavoury or sun-soaked and wind-swept. Everything is seen, however, through the keen eyes and the bare, monosyllabic and poverty-stricken language of Bill, and this language is consistently used not only in set conversational pieces but in description of mood and background as well. The New Zealand idiom, or at any rate *one* of the New Zealand idioms, becomes expressive in a way no other writer has achieved, and it is the

idiom of common utterance, which is so fully reproduced by
Sargeson that it becomes akin to poetic utterance.

By the time my second payday came around I was well sick of
working for the Dally. He was certainly tough to work for. He was
tight with the hot water; and it was hard to make a job of the dishes
when there was grease floating thick on the top of a sink full of dirty
water. And there were things I saw that put me right off the tucker.
If the pumpkin wouldn't cook the cook'd put it out on a big dish
and work it through his fingers until he'd squeezed all the lumps out.
And a man hardly had time to wipe off his own sweat, let alone roll
a cigarette, so for a spell I used to go out the back and pretend to do
a job for myself. But I couldn't do that too often, because if there
wasn't any cleaning up to do there was always the spuds to keep
ahead with. You had to put them in a machine and turn the handle
to knock the worst of the skin off, and with the weather like it was it
certainly made a man sweat doing the turning.[8]

The scenes at the police station, the Court and the gaol are
memorable, though not primarily because they give a detailed
and vivid picture of part of the social environment that is never
very far outside the consciousness of people like Bill, constitu-
tionally incapable of living a respectable suburban life. Sargeson
is rarely interested in describing the background of his characters for its own sake. He gives no sign here any more than he
does in the hospital scenes or at the medical examination, which
Bill has to undergo to discover if he is able to do relief work,
that he is intent on drawing the reader into sordid or unpleasant
areas as a form of fictional slumming. The scenes themselves
are a natural outcome of the plot, convincingly functional in
terms of Bill's attitudes. They become an extension of his personality, a window from which to view the way in which his
mind and emotions work:

. . . they took me downstairs and turned me over to a john who wrote
my name down in a book and told me to hand in all my money, but
there was nothing doing because I didn't have any. Then when he'd
taken my belt off me (it was so as I couldn't hang myself I suppose),
he took me along a passage and locked me up. I sat down to save
myself from holding my pants up, and I was sitting there thinking
how it was the first time I'd ever been in one of those places, when

the john came back with a tray that was loaded up with a big dinner. It was a real good dinner too, two courses and plenty to eat, and I could have eaten the lot and more, but I thought gee, so far as tucker goes I'm better off than poor old Terry is. I might be anyhow, I thought, because I remembered I didn't know whether he'd got any money out of Reg. All the same I didn't like to think of Terry going hungry, so I tore some pages out of a Western that was in the cell, and wrapped up half of both courses and put the parcel in my pocket. All in together it certainly looked an awful mess, but I thought Terry wouldn't mind if he was feeling empty.[9]

The reviewer of the *Collected Stories* in the *Times Literary Supplement* referred to the New Zealand world, to the Sargeson world that is reflected in them, by commenting on it as "a sad and savage world";[10] but this is to place too great an emphasis on the impotence and impoverishment of the human spirit contained in much of his work, and far too little emphasis on the gaiety and wit that are also highly characteristic of his writing. It is worth remembering that one of the questions he has been asked continually is "Why are you always joking, why do you persist in being cheerful over serious matters?" In life as in art Sargeson is more frequently than otherwise light-hearted, and it is not difficult to discover a rich vein of comedy in his work, although some forms of wry humour that he is accustomed to exploit may occasionally jar or be misinterpreted by oversensitive readers. In the extract just quoted a series of conflicting emotions is involved, but it is effective for other reasons than those associated with the wretchedness and uncertainty of Bill's situation or with his sympathy with others in a like predicament. We realize that through the midst of the colloquial language used there emerges a portrait of a hard but at the same time enormously sympathetic and gay realist, subject to many varying moods but concerned mainly with his quite irrational affection for Terry, whom he may have left without a cobber, without a mate willing and able to care for him and attend to his elementary needs. The passage continues a little later:

. . and maybe it was because of the way those beds creaked that I couldn't get to sleep. They didn't stop creaking, and I thought maybe they were jokers like me who'd been locked up for the first time. It

made me start thinking about what makes a man get tough and land
himself in clink. Because all those jokers must have been the same
as I was once too, just kids. And I started to remember about when
I was a kid. I remembered the times when I'd get a kick on the
behind for pinching out of the bin where they threw the rotten fruit
along at the auction mart in the town where I lived. And the times
when the old man would come home tight, and us kids'd go out in
the morning and find him lying in the onion bed without hardly
a stitch on. And I remembered other times too, and I never thought
about Terry or Maggie much. I just couldn't take my mind off the
jokers that were locked up alongside me, because their beds never
left off creaking all night.[11]

Sargeson's method of narration becomes something that is not
far removed from an extended interior monologue, but a monologue that is concerned with external objects and impressions
rather than with feelings and half-uttered thoughts. These are
communicated to the reader more by the rhythm and movement
of language than by any private confession or unequivocal
statement; the result of the method is that the other characters
never fully materialize as individuals, but only as subjects of
Bill's regard or attention. He himself is innocent of any capacity
to judge, to analyze or to penetrate beyond the rough external
surfaces of his acquaintances, and they remain as shadowy
figures in the background of his emotions and imagination. All
that he knows about them can be summed up in the remark:
"everybody must be pretty much the same in most ways if you
could only find out." Even Terry appears enigmatical and obscure; and since the reader can know only as much as Bill knows
about him the core of his personality is as inaccessible as his
feelings. Bill never knows and therefore the reader can never
know whether after Reg's handsome win at the races Terry
deserted Bill for a few crucial days in the effort to obtain an
illegitimate share of the money. Bill never knows and therefore
the reader can never know whether their relationship is completely one-sided and its story becomes one of unrequited or
at best ambiguous love. The last scenes rise skilfully to their
not wholly unexpected and touching climax. After the abortive
trial the extraordinary guileless but not always innocent Bill is
at last discharged because Maggie reverses her evidence. This

has been brought about by the absent Terry, who with his knowledge of the world and its ways has easily recognized that Maggie is no woman but the catamite of the burly "Mr. Popeye the sailorman." On his release he finds that the consumptive Terry has been carried off to a hospital, and in a bizarre and hilariously pathetic episode proceeds to "rescue" him and trundle him off at night in a wheelbarrow to die under his tender ministrations at the Clegg boarding house.

In the scene beside Terry's deathbed Bill's dread of loneliness and desire for comradeship are submerged in a completely self-less and inarticulate devotion which becomes a triumph of understatement:

I'd look at him lying there.
Terry, I'd say.
What is it boy? he'd say.
Nothing, I'd say.
And then I'd say, Terry.
And instead of answering he'd just have a sort of faint grin on his face.
Terry, I'd say.
But I never could get any further than just saying Terry.
I wanted to say something but I didn't know what it was and I couldn't say it.
Terry, I'd say.
And he'd sort of grin. And sometimes I'd take his hand and hold it tight, and he'd let it stay in my hand, and there'd be the faint grin on his face.
Terry, I'd say.
I'm all right boy, he'd say.
And sometimes I couldn't stand it, I'd have to just rush off and leave him there.[12]

The final comment on what some critics have all too easily taken to be a disguised but simple homosexual theme is given after Terry's death, when Bill goes out and along the street to a taxi driver with whom he had previously won a double.

Do you want to take one? he said.
No, I said, and I'd only got a few bob, but I asked him if he knew of any decent sheilas.

He grinned and put away the paper he was reading and told me
to hop in.

You surprise me, he said.

And it was a fine warm night for a drive. Maybe if only it had
rained, I remember I thought.[13]

III   *Mateship*

There are qualities in *That Summer* and in the short stories
that extend beyond the purely literary art of fictional writing
into the social phenomenon and historical truth of what has
been called "Mateship." "That's one thing the slump did," says
the narrator of *A Man and his Wife*. "It put a certain sort of
comradeship into life that you don't find now." It was not, however, the slump alone that encouraged a form of masculine
comradeship. The conditions of life, particularly in Australia
and New Zealand, countries far away from the older civiliza-
tions, led to a sometimes exaggerated emphasis on the loyalty
that might exist between man and man. Mateship is a dominant
theme that runs through the writing of Joseph Furphy, Henry
Lawson and many other writers of Australian prose and verse,
especially those associated with the nineties of the last century;
and it is not without significance that Sargeson has expressed
a considerable interest in Lawson's work. This is not to suggest
that the qualities of mateship so apparent in his writing have
been in any way derived from across the Tasman. That they
were reinforced is probable, because the interest in Australian
literature, in the ballads and short stories of Lawson for example,
was widespread throughout New Zealand during the nineties
and the early decades of the present century. There were many
factors that contributed to this antipodean conception of mateship—the necessary camaraderie of the bush and the gold
diggings, the isolation and comparative absence of feminine
company, the rise of trade unions and the struggle for better
conditions, the history of the Anzacs during World War I and
the drawing together of men on relief work during the great
depression. Although insufficient exploration has yet been made
into the origins and implications of mateship, there is enough
evidence to indicate that Professor Murdoch, commenting on the

familiar inquiry, "Got a match, mate?", was right to see in it something that can be regarded as an expression of an Australian (or New Zealand) ideal, a "casual free and easy, good-humoured mateship," [14] an outward sign of a rough-and-ready democratic attitude that, temporarily at least, rises above class barriers and social pretensions of rank or income.

Sargeson's world is largely a male world, and one in which his Bills and Teds and Sams and Freds tend to move about in pairs, their virtues being virtues of loyalty to a masculine code, their vices being vices of disloyalty to that code. When Bill in *That Summer* is sitting near Terry who is sleeping in a park with his hat over his face, he is approached by a man who wants to borrow a few bob and tell him a story of how he'd been let down by a mate:

> It just shows you, he said.
> Yes, I said.
> A man wants a mate that won't let him down, he said.
> Yes, I said. But I wasn't paying much attention because Terry had woke up.
> I've got to go, I said.
> Wait a minute mate, he said.
> No, I said, I've got to go.
> Listen mate, he said.
> No sorry, I said, and I went back to Terry.[15]

Much later in the story when Bill had taken Terry from the hospital and was looking after him at the Cleggs, he walked down to the waterfront wondering what he could do to supplement his day and a half's relief work. He falls into conversation with a young fellow who tells him that he is going to a farming job to break in twenty-five acres of rough land:

> He told me all about it, and if there wasn't any catch it sounded as if there might be something in it. So I told him the jobs I'd had on farms.
> Well, he said, how about being mates and going together?
> And I liked the look of him so I said O.K. right off, and the thought of being back working on the land again made me feel suddenly all worked up. But next minute I remembered, so I said wait on a bit, because I'd need longer time to decide.[16]

He had, of course, remembered Terry and his greater loyalty
to a cobber who was lying in bed awaiting his return.

It is this conception of mateship that underlies so many of
Sargeson's short stories, and sometimes seems the only ethical
value that remains among the inarticulate toughs and outcasts
that inhabit his New Zealand world; but because they are incapable of sustained thought and their sensitivity is buried
beneath layers of protective covering, the expression of such an
abstract ideal is usually beyond their powers. They manifest their
longing for communion in personal, restricted and masculine
terms, as an instinctive groping towards a free and easy but an
equal relationship with their fellows, a desire rather than a
reality. When it is destroyed or betrayed, as in such stories as
A Great Day, I've Lost my Pal, or *A Pair of Socks,* when it is
in danger of being destroyed or betrayed, as it always is in *That
Summer,* the pathos has overtones that are related to the failure
of the belief in human brotherhood. There are also homosexual
overtones, but these are neither forced nor insistent. Sargeson's
interest in exclusively male situations and his avoidance of any
treatment of fulfilled human love between a man and a woman
are the consequence of his preoccupation with mateship as a
way of life in a world where tenderness is not the rule but the
exception.

It may seem curious that up to the time of writing *That
Summer* his attempts to dramatize the loneliness of the human
heart and its yearning for relationship and love, his exploration
of the simplicities of behaviour among the deprived and uncouth
had taken no account of the Maori. Here, it might be suggested,
was rich material waiting to be used if the doctrine of the Noble
Savage needed to be invoked; and certain aspects of mateship
are indeed closely associated with a modern restatement of that
doctrine. However, there had been too many writers intent on
sentimentalizing the Maori character for one who was concerned
not only with catching the tones of the *pakeha* New Zealand
voice, but in exploring the social morality of the European who
had become identified with the country, to extend his range into
an area so obvious and yet unsuitable for his particular purposes.
Only in *White Man's Burden* had Sargeson casually introduced
some Maoris. Its scene is set in a lonely pub on a road up north:

"A lot more Maoris came in and a few white chaps. Gosh, Bill was right. They were rough, rougher than the Maoris," [17] but although one or two of them had an air of refinement, the narrator who spent the night in a shed not far from the bar was kept awake by the tremendous noise, and reflects: "Gosh, there's a great day coming for Abyssinia when civilization gets properly going there."

At this time Sargeson evidently had no wish to glorify the magnanimous Maori whose manner of living can sometimes provide such a scathing indictment of European civilization. He confined himself to the Noble Savage in the shape of the casual European worker, because he was primarily interested in the moral climate of a semi-urbanized society which had already turned its back on freedom, spontaneity, and human brotherhood in order to stress the false values of standardization and respectability. If Sargeson can be accused of encouraging, at least by implication, the cult of the primitive, it cannot easily be maintained that he has chosen illegitimate means to emphasize the pattern of experiences to which he has devoted his attention. Human brotherhood may sometimes prove to be a hazy creed, but it is not an insignificant one, and *That Summer* can fairly be regarded as the climax of Sargeson's career as a writer of short stories. Within it is contained much of what he was aiming for and meaning—his stress on the loneliness and isolation of the human being at all times and in all places, his recognition of the intense need and desire for human affection and comradeship, his suspicion of the ready-made and stereotyped conventionality that is frequently associated with a formalized education and a routine job, his conviction that the rudimentary spiritual life of the outcasts of society is more valuable than the subtleties of the sophisticated, and his awareness that kindness of heart is of greater importance than articulate utterance.

CHAPTER 5

The Pilgrim's Role

"It might be Apollyon's world, but it was mine too."

I Search for a Hero

ALTHOUGH by the early forties Sargeson had achieved a considerable reputation that was not confined to New Zealand, and by the time of the *Collected Stories* an Australian reviewer was prepared to place him among "the incontestably great short story writers" [1] in the Anglo-Saxon world, it does not follow that such a writer can produce an effective and powerful novel. The taut but fragmentary medium which he had devised to suit his own needs might prove unsatisfactory for an extended work of fiction, for it might tend to disintegrate into a series of only partly connected glimpses of the New Zealand life he was anxious to explore. Nevertheless, he had not abandoned the idea of continuing with the programme which even at an early age he had firmly fixed in his mind, and to which he had returned again and again. He might find it necessary to create a new medium and a more flexible structure in order to contain his expanded vision of what seemed to him important elements of New Zealand life. His work had all been experimental and would continue to be experimental, not because he now lacked confidence or had been unable to learn from his struggle with material, form, and language, but because the absence of a New Zealand tradition made it inevitable and essential that a writer should feel his way and discover how to shape experience according to the requirements of the kind of world in which he had been born and chosen to remain.

What he had gained from his early writings was a realization that he could almost at will adopt the mask of another personality, whether as a character or as narrator, and adopt it so readily and so completely that at times he was able to feel that his own identity had been destroyed. He spoke with the voices of others; he lived in scenes which were not his own; and yet in some peculiar way these characters and scenes were part of his own being. His personal experiences had gone through such a process of imaginative transformation that what emerged was something that bore little relation to them except in unimportant details. From a private world of his own he had been able to enter into the freedom of a larger and public world of the imagination. By losing, by sacrificing his identity, he had found the multiple identity familiar to the creative artist. As a consequence he had discovered that the language and the structure of the sentences he used were quite distinct from his own ways of expression and his own natural voice. He was writing in an idiom that belonged to his characters and, through them, to the New Zealanders of whom they were the fictional representatives.

In a sense he had created an artificial language, but artificial only in that it was used consistently and with art. It was not that all or many New Zealanders spoke in the voices that Sargeson used, but rather that through these voices could be heard the characteristic tones and vocabulary of New Zealanders. His broadcast discussion "Writing a Novel" was to show his intense awareness of the importance of language; but from his years of experimenting with the short story had come a facility in the choice of words and the selection of phrase which showed at least that he had overcome his earlier clumsiness and his addiction to inappropriate models. His ear was now a competent organ for the modulation of tone and meaning. Nevertheless, "Writing a Novel" suggested that for a long time he had been concerned with the problem of the fictional New Zealand "hero" and with the quality of New Zealand life, that he had been trying to think things out in order to determine more accurately the kind of novel he had every intention of writing: "like Byron at the beginning of Don Juan," he wrote, "I felt the need of a suitable hero, and wanted if possible to avoid any suggestion that the author himself was the hero, as is rather common in novels these days. I wondered whether my failure to find a suitable hero was a shortcoming of my own or a shortcoming of this material of New Zealand life that I was so determined to deal with." His search for a hero was closely bound up not with any shortcomings that were personal to him alone, but with the conviction that had only strengthened through the years that there were certain aspects of New Zealand life that required concentrated attention if they were to be given adequate fictional form.

By the early forties several New Zealand writers had already begun to turn to the novel in order to try to capture some of the characteristics of the land and the people: John A. Lee whose *Children of the Poor* (1934), a partly autobiographical social exposure of poverty and prostitution in Dunedin, had aroused much excited and uninformed criticism; Robin Hyde, whose brief series of novels really concluded in 1938 with *The Godwits Fly;* and John Mulgan, whose *Man Alone,* published in 1939, still remains one of the finest of New Zealand novels. None of these authors, however, had been primarily concerned with the ideas with which Sargeson was preoccupied. As his biography indicates he was wrapped up in a dream of reality, the New Zealand reality, which was symbolized for him by the tall feathery shape of a wild honeysuckle tree and the prison of a narrow sectarian belief. It was symbolized by the prison of the senses and the life of the senses, "a pure and shameless life," that he was able to live when as he climbed Te Aroha he temporarily abandoned his pilgrim's role and ceased to care that it was Apollyon's world. It was a world that was also his, a world that belonged to a living sentient human being.

He had come to the conclusion that the only way to understand New Zealand and important aspects of the New Zealand character, the only way to explore the quality of New Zealand life was to begin with the soul-destroying disease of puritanism and to pursue those forgotten or obscured values which, like an earlier paganism, can be derived more easily from close contact with the soil and its life-giving attributes. Such ideas carry buried within them the seeds of a sentimentalism similar to that contained in the doctrine of the Noble Savage. The rejection of an urban civilization with all its suppression of what used to be called "natural" instincts, the adherence to a different and more elastic creed expressed by Blake in his comment, "damn braces, bless relaxes," can lead to a modern but equally vague version of the pastoral. Such attitudes can be wholly salutary, however, if they cast doubts on the divine right of the puritan to build a world in his own image, and affirm the freedom of the individual to follow his generous impulses in order to find joy in living and creating.

What Sargeson was doing in his own way and from his own experience of growing up in New Zealand was parallel to the work that had been produced by many modern novelists. As man in his long pilgrimage through time has become immersed in the multiplicity of gadgets with which he has surrounded himself, and has lost all sense of direction, he has tended to find comfort in the artificial rules and regulations that he has devised in order to create an illusion of security, and has forgotten the fundamental truth hidden in the psalmist's injunction: "I will lift up mine eyes unto the hills, from whence cometh my help." Hence it is that many of the more significant writers of fiction and poetry have been insistent on drawing attention to the cleavage between an ossified social structure that can mean death to the spirit and the attempts to discover a way of life in which and through which man's sensuous appreciation of all aspects of living may be able to grow and develop. In parable and extended narrative form E. M. Forster has not been alone in his concern to draw the contrast between two ways of life which in *The Longest Journey* he has denominated as Sawston and Wiltshire, between the closed-in environment of those who have ceased to explore and the open downs with the dry turf and the scent of thyme. Such methods of writing which depend on the imagination and intuitive perception of the reader, because threads of symbolism are interwoven with the narrative, can be disturbing to those who are suspicious of any attempt to arouse them out of their comfortable refuge of acceptable platitudes. They prefer direct to imaginative realism. They expect to find the whole meaning on the surface. They do not want to reexamine their assumptions about life or to be forced to read a novel at more than one level.

Sargeson had made a distinct break with the past, with the methods and themes of his short stories, although it is true to say that much of what he was attempting to communicate in *I Saw in My Dream* had already been implicit in them. Nevertheless, he was expanding and enriching what has been called "the Sargeson world" and, as was necessary, developing a structure more suited to the form of the novel. As with many of his

illustrious predecessors in other countries his subject began to
shape itself into the story of a young man growing up and
freeing himself from the ghosts of the past, discovering his own
identity and attempting to escape from a world which was
suffocating to the spirit and not of his own making. It was
almost predetermined for him, as for many writers of first novels,
that he should be concerned with flight and escape, with the
discomfort of emergence from the womb and the unconscious
desire to return to its safety, with the continual threat of spiritual entombment and with the uncertain search for a place of
refuge or a cave of retreat. But, although from *Great Expectations* to *Tono-Bungay*, from *The Ordeal of Richard Feverel* to
Sons and Lovers, from *Pendennis* to *A Portrait of the Artist as
a Young Man*, the pilgrim's progress of a human being from
adolescence to early manhood, from swathing bands to emanci-
pation, had been a constant theme among many variables, Sargeson's chronicle of departure from the chrysalis had its own
characteristically New Zealand features. These were largely the
consequence of a distortion of the original puritanism that had
developed through the nineteenth century and early decades of
the twentieth century and had its parallels in most of the newer
countries, in the United States as well as in Australia. It was
a distortion which as Sargeson expressed it tended "to think of
the Christian religion not as something that is good, but as
something that is goody-goody," [2] and led to a family life and
a wider public life that frequently attempted to "regulate human
conduct by a system of rigid prohibitions." His attraction to the
novels of Hawthorne and Mark Twain is easy to understand.
There was also, however, and outside this restricted and con-
forming life, a world of mountain and gully, of bush and river-
bed, a whole world empty and waiting, a sunlit world which
prompted the thought that came into the mind of the central
character in *I Saw in My Dream*: "he had somehow got himself
lost in some sort of a cave, with no hope of ever being able
to find a way out." [3]

The title he chose for his novel had all the implications of
a dream of reality as well as of a fervent puritanical belief which
found in the doctrine of original sin ample warrant for rejecting
and denouncing the normal impulses of human beings for a rich

and sensitive life in the world of the here and now. It had implications of flight and escape, of deceitful havens of refuge, of paths to be avoided and of the pilgrim's journey to find a way around the slough of despondency. Bunyan's allegory was an essential part of the tradition of the true sectarian, and although it could provide a dangerous model for any writer, it might offer images for the kind of novel Sargeson was bent on writing. The frequently repeated phrase "Then I saw in my dream . . ." could take him back to the time when he too had imagined himself to be a pilgrim preparing to enter the Eternal City. It could take him back to the time when he had attempted to explain to his uncle the nature of the evangelical mission towards which his Bible class camp had inspired him, while outside on the skyline the great honeysuckle tree was waiting as a symbol of growth and of hope in the future. In "I believe . . ." E. P. Dobson has pointed out the following passage as one of special significance in relation to *I Saw in My Dream*. Christian is passing through the Valley of the Shadow of Death, and Bunyan relates:

Now I saw in my Dream, that at the end of this Valley lay blood, bones, ashes, and mangled bodies of men, even of Pilgrims that had gone this way formerly; And while I was musing what should be the reason, I espied a little before me a Cave, where two Giants, *Pope* and *Pagan*, dwelt in old time, by whose Power and Tyranny the Men whose bones, blood, ashes, etc., lay there, were cruelly put to death. But by this place *Christian* went without much danger, whereat I somewhat wondered: but I have learnt since, that *Pagan* has been dead many a day; and as for the other, though he be yet alive, he is by reason of age, and also of the many shrewd brushes that he met with in his younger dayes, grown so crazy and stiff in his joynts, that he can now do little more then sit in his Caves mouth, grinning at Pilgrims as they go by, and biting his nails, because he cannot come at them.[4]

In so far as this passage is relevant to the meaning and organization of Sargeson's novel it is possible to read the allegory in a way that could not have been palatable either to the seventeenth century or later puritans. The doctrine of the giant *Pope* had become obsolete as far as Bunyan was concerned and had been replaced by a form of Calvinistic belief that nourished the souls of the elect, the true believers; but *Pagan* was dead, and in spite of Bunyan's evident appreciation of the beauties of the countryside he seemed to be content for man to sever the links that joined his sensuous being to the rich inheritance of the past. He had become a vessel into which could be poured the exhortations of the pious and those who adhered to a strict faith, a vessel to be saved from the burning, a wayward traveller who must be directed to the true path that would lead through the Valley of the Shadow of Death and past the cave where in earlier days *Pagan* had lived. Nevertheless, Sargeson had experienced the time when he had been "suddenly and miraculously permitted" to live "the pure life of the senses." He had learnt from Pascal "that there is nothing man may not make natural, nor anything natural he may not lose," and he knew that the rigid, spirit-destroying prohibitions of a decayed puritanism must be abandoned in order to come to a state of life affirmation and not of life denial.

It is only at the end of *I Saw in My Dream,* in the brief third section, that the central character is able to say "Yes" to life and to the hopeful prospect of human creativeness. Sargeson's use of italicized passages is a convenient but disturbing device to indicate an interior monologue bordering on delirium, an almost trance-like condition in which the compulsive reflections of a young man burst forth into what Carlyle would have called an "Everlasting No" to life, a descent into an "indefinite and pining fear," a quivering and timorous guilt-ridden attitude to life as to a devouring monster and a shrinking back to the lost but warm comfort of the womb. Woven through the narrative, particularly of the first section, is a series of agonizing negatives, a refusal to accept life in terms of natural instincts and sensuous experience—*"no please no God please."* By the end of *I Saw in My Dream* the same boy, now in his early manhood, is able not only to murmur an italicized *"yes"* but to follow it with a capitalized and resounding repetition of the same affirmative, a Carlylese "Everlasting Yea," without the connotations given to it by that advocate of silence and work, that celebrated Calvinist who somewhere along the road had mislaid his creed. It is a

"YES" not unlike Molly Bloom's final utterance from her slumbering world at the end of Joyce's *Ulysses*.

II *When the Wind Blows*

The first section of the novel was originally issued as a separate publication in 1945 under the title of *When the Wind Blows*, carrying with it implications of the lullaby and the fall both of the cradle and of the baby from the treetop. At the time it was impossible to catch more than a glimpse of Sargeson's intentions in the completed work, which was published in 1949 with its final title of *I Saw in My Dream*. This method of publication lends colour to the suggestion that at the beginning the novel had not been conceived as a whole, and the relations of its parts to the finished product had been so inadequately worked out that there remained the uneasy feeling that the second and much longer section had been added to rather than absorbed by the structure, and that the third brief section was something in the nature of an afterthought or epilogue. Nevertheless, this awkward arrangement of a pilgrim's progress of a New Zealander has a logic of its own which becomes apparent when the reader is able to forget his preconceived ideas and accept it as an experimental work of great integrity.

The first section, that which bore the early title of *When the Wind Blows*, is divided into twelve chapters or subsections, each of which gives a fleeting glimpse of Henry Griffiths from his childhood to post-adolescence. Although there are constant reminders that Sargeson's first attempt at a novel was modelled on Joyce's *Portrait of the Artist as a Young Man*, it is evident that as D'Arcy Cresswell, writing from England, said: "its first four chapters, with their masculine clarity and objectiveness, their transparent thinness, are incomparably the finest creative writing which has come out of New Zealand, not excepting anything of Katharine Mansfield's";[5] but what was more important for local tradition was that the method he had adopted was not only the best but the most advisable. As in his short stories he continued to refuse to comment on his characters or to obtrude his own opinions. He chose the way of indirect narration, significantly, as the same critic has stressed, for "it's a native art we are after. The first New Zealander, like the last huia, requires wary stalking in difficult country to get a sight of him. . . . It's best at first just to eavesdrop; understanding and interpretation come later." [6] These first four chapters are episodic and compressed, in the way the short story writer almost inevitably proceeds; but the episodes are linked by the small boy's growing awareness of the narrow, private world which continually engrosses his attention and of the necessity to retreat headlong into the protective safety of his mother's arms. It is also sterile because there is nothing in it to excite or to satisfy his curiosity or his feeble attempts to understand the kind of world into which he has emerged. He clings to the security of his early childhood, to that timeless experience stretching forward and backward into the same static existence, for

"It had always been so, and it would never be any different because you had never noticed any change. There was just mother and father, and auntie Clara and Arnold your brother, who was older than you and went to school, but he had always gone to school, and they said you would go to school too, someday. Someday. That would be a long, long time, because just one day was a long, long time, and when mother said, It's your bedtime now, you never wanted to go, because it was such a long, long time until the next day." [7]

The dreamlike quality that pervades so much of *When the Wind Blows* is intensified by the comparative lack of action and the distancing of Henry and his family, so that everything is seen through a veil of Sargeson's own making, and the small boy is always trying, though vainly, to re-enter that certain and secure retreat with which the book opens,

> Who loves you?
> Mummy and daddy.
> Who else?
> Auntie Clara.
> And who else?
> Gentle Jesus
> And who else?

> Our Father which art in heaven . . .
> And when that was over mother said,
> *Goodnight, sweet repose*
> *All the bed, and all the clothes,*

and she kissed you and took away the candle, and you were left in the dark, warm in the hollow of the bed, *snug as a bug in a rug.*[8]

In this opening is to be found the source of some of the refrains that wind their way through the book, in particular the refrain of the snug retreat from the complexities of the world. For in moments of difficulty, of uncertainty or of bewildered guilt, Henry's morbid imagination gathers together detached portions of his experience and neurotically reassembles them in an unspoken and semi-conscious interior monologue, while his whole being yearns for the warm hollow of his bed and a pre-natal comfort. His early years at school, fragmentary and disconnected as they are, are nevertheless carefully patterned in order to reveal a current of subconscious and conflicting feelings as he finds himself adrift in a strange and horrifying world. One of his school companions observes that "a kid that was tied to his old woman's apron strings oughtn't to be allowed to go to school. Because he might wet his pants." [9] A fight in a gravel pit between two boys is preceded by the unexpected sight in the nearby saleyards of a cow giving birth to a calf; and there becomes associated in his mind his schoolmate with "his mouth open and his tongue hanging out and the blood running down" [10] and the cow "lying on her side in the muck, all the time making a soft mooing sound, her eyes big and staring, her four legs stretched out and moving, and another leg that didn't move, just one more, sticking out from the back of her. And the muck red with blood all round her." [11] And as he goes on his first holiday and is saying goodbye to his mother his fearful imagination conjures up a possible motor accident and "*the motor car was coming no please no time to cross in front no mother had to wear her glasses the motor car was oh please and mother and the wheels going up and down bump! bang! oh! and blood no please no.*" [12] At moments of crisis such fragments of isolated experience are drawn together and produce an hysterical compound of fears, guilts and longings to retreat. Much later in the book when Henry is suffering what amounts to a nervous break-down, the movement of his mind is rendered in the following incoherent phrases:

oh crybaby, crybaby, running home from school, crybaby, boys that were tied to their mothers' apron strings wet their pants in school. Crybaby. Mother had to wear her glasses and didn't see oh oh, oh my finger and Knocky had his tongue cut and the blood dripped and ran down, and you ran home safe to mother. You didn't tell, you didn't oh no, but you ran home safe to mother and nothing could hurt you then. And mother was safe too, after all the blood, blood dripping and running, the muck all red round the cow with that leg sticking out behind oh no. Because, because just because. Because what? Because I couldn't help it. But you MUST help it, a big boy like you, you're not a baby any more, you're getting a big boy now. To think after all these years, after all I've done for you, I couldn't bring you up CLEAN.[13]

In each of the first four subsections, and continuing through-out *When the Wind Blows*, there are slight incidents which dis-close Henry's "natural" or, according to the point of view, his "unhealthy" preoccupation with sex. Indeed this, the first part of Sargeson's novel, is largely concerned with what the author evidently regards a dominant feature of New Zealand life, im-ported as it has been, and made more monstrous in the process, from a puritanism which in the nineteenth century had degen-erated into a system of prohibitions that was fundamentally life-denying. He is concerned with the immense harm that the sup-pression of normal impulses and curiosity can cause to the minds and outlook of young people. This is no new theme for the modern novelist; it is new only in that it is given the typical small-town background of a provincial New Zealand setting and that the characters, in so far as they are permitted to materialize sufficiently, are authentic New Zealanders. It is new only be-cause the writer brings a different technique, a different range of assumptions and experiences to his task; but he uses the methods of the novelist and not those of the zealous reformer and sociologist. His aim was not to write a psychological case history of his youthful protagonist, but to bring to life a facet of human experience that could illuminate the behaviour pat-

terns of a large proportion of his fellow countrymen. By means
of his consistent but indirect monologue he was intent on dram-
atizing and revealing the warped soul of an ordinary New Zealander who had been exposed not to a series of spectacular
adventures nor to the baneful influence of what is usually called
a bad social or family environment, but to a self-righteous and
narrow domestic life that is completely unimaginative, wholly
destructive to the emotional responses of an average adolescent.

Without a phrase of commentary or any authorial intrusion
the book becomes a damning indictment of the inhibitory consequences of sexual repression. Henry moves in a world that is
obscurely erotic and secretly fascinating. As a very small child
he watches his mother "inside her nightgown, all except her
head, the sleeves hanging empty, and bit by bit mother's clothes
went inside the nightgown, until she took it off and she was
standing there with all her clothes on." [14] He accompanies his
father each morning to feed the fowls and knows that if he is
lucky he might "see the rooster get on top of one of the chooks
and give it a hiding." He goes to stay with his aunt and cousin
Cherry, who early on the last morning climbs into bed with him
and, while she hugs and kisses him, he remains terrified and
flustered and longing for the moment when the kettle will boil
and she will vanish to make a cup of tea for her mother. Always the growing boy is surrounded by symbols and incidents
of sexual significance, whether these are concerned with the
smutty rhymes and riddles of his playmates or his abortive attempt outside the bathroom window to see his aunt Clara within,
and his mother's uncomprehending exclamation as she hit him
again and again and cried "After all the years I've tried to do
my best for you . . . to think I couldn't bring you up *clean*." [15]
Of course she had tried to the best of her meagre ability, as the
little manual that she left in his room indicated, *"no no the book
he found on his bed that afternoon after school, mother must
have left it there and it was a hard job trying to look her in the
face for days, birds flowers and the 'shining creature' a girl who
said I have kept myself pure for you, and he said and I for you,
and you could get diseases worse than leprosy, yes and secret
vice please NO."* [16] This frightening accent placed upon "purity"
and the mysteries of sex by the sectarian mind, not in terms of

understanding, imaginative sympathy, and open acknowledge-
ment, but of reticence and bewildering innuendo, fills the boy's
mind with the corroding fear that ideas or actions even remotely
sexual in their import will cause him to be damned forever and
unloved forever.

The later childhood of Henry begins with his nightly withdrawal into the closed circle of unintimate family life. This is
snug seclusion of the family, which for so long has been a New
Zealand fetish, without any recognition that outside it lies the
jungle of thoughts and impulses which are an essential part of
the growing boy's life.

. . . and then what had been so wished for and looked forward to
came true. That something perfect took the shape of a ball, or so
it would seem now and then. You lived inside the ball, and it was
lovely to have it all round you, you lived contented right inside at
the centre. There was room for you by the fire, there was only
father and mother, auntie Clara went to bed early, and Arnold went
out always and never said where he went. Anyhow there was room
for you there by the fire, room for your easy chair and father's and
mother's, mother with her ball of wool doing her darning, and
father reading the newspaper. With your soft slippers on you could
even put your feet up near the mantelpiece without having anything
said. And with the heat of the fire on your legs you could read
your book, not trash, you weren't allowed to read that, but Edward
S. Ellis was all right. The Hunter of the Ozarks, The Lost Trail,
The Last Warpath, Deerfoot was in every one of them, and from
inside that ball where you lived contented, you looked out. . . . [17]

Outside the ball, however, was a chaotic world of which, scared
and trembling though he was, his cousin Cherry had given him
an exciting but needlessly guilty moment of insight. Another of
a different kind was caused by a young tramp, turned away by
Henry on instructions from his father, but entertained by his
brother Arnold.

It is at this point and for the first time in the novel that the
reader becomes aware of a disproportion between episodes and
theme, for as the episodes increase in length the density of the
material is reduced, and the author draws back from elaborating
on hints of character portrayal and of possible incident in order
to continue circling round the mind and emotions of the closed-in

Henry. His brother Arnold and the tramp remain as shadowy intrusions into the theme. The long episode concerned with the visit of his rough and profane uncles and Henry's temptation to play tennis on a Sunday morning instead of completing his paper on "Ye are my friends if ye do whatsoever I command you" becomes undramatic and banal. His meeting with Marge at the opening of the tennis club remains irrelevant and insignificant until the threads are picked up in the later portion of the second section. It is as though Sargeson has been caught between the difficulties of the novel and those of the short story, between the hazards of the elaborated episode and the significant glimpses of mind and attitude in a restricted space, a dilemma which he was able to overcome more successfully later in the novel. Even the impact of the extended seventh subsection, which provides *When the Wind Blows* with its traumatic climax, its point of reference to which the earlier and later subsections all relate, becomes blunted because Henry's conversation with the girl in the lonely law office is directed towards incidents that never develop, and hampers without greatly illuminating the reader's perception of Henry's disturbed state of mind.

Nevertheless, it is in this office, abandoned for long periods by the alcoholic lawyer, their employer, when boy and girl are left together for hours during the day, that a symbolic enactment, a disastrous parody of Henry's domestic situation takes place. The soft ball of contentment, the refuge of his childhood, in which he had formerly curled up in the evenings at home, is now represented by the legal strong-room in which he temporarily locks his companion to protect her from lascivious workmen who chat with her through the window, to save her for himself and to relieve him of his undetermined and unacknowledged desires. Although the italicized and neurotic interior monologue makes it plain to the reader, Henry does not realize that his whole development has been conditioned by the locking up of his own instincts and feelings within a closed cell, from which he finds it impossible to escape. Later, in a spasm of unreasoning and abnormal fear, he thinks:

. . . and now he might be going to get LOCKED UP HIMSELF.
Five years. Oh no no. He'd better tell mother and father. But say

they didn't believe him, say they thought he HAD done something,
and because he was feeling guilty and frightened he was telling lies?
Say father went and spoke to the girl's father oh no no. And say
the girl was asked and said oh no. Because if mother and father
thought he had done something what would they do? He'd get the
worst hiding he'd ever had in his life. Yes of course. But what else?
That time he'd looked through the key hole yes, and mother had
said if he was a few years older he'd have deserved to be LOCKED
UP FOR THE REST OF HIS LIFE oh no please God no you
mustn't let. But nobody was going to tell and nothing was going to
happen of course.[18]

Passages such as this look forward to the second long section of
the novel, which will be concerned with the projected walling
up of Cedric in a cave high on the hillside behind his parents'
farm and with the psychological cave in which Henry-David had
become lost and could find no way out. It is connected even with
the undeveloped episode of the opening of the tennis courts
at which the emancipated Marge is for a brief time locked in
the lavatory, and someone comments: "Now, whoever would do
a childish thing like that." [19]

There are many readers who are liable to be impatient with
these slight indications of symbolism; and the success of the
novel as distinct from a series of vivid impressions must finally
depend on whether or not Henry's character and predicament
are so firmly established in the early part of the book as to convince us of the validity of the symbolic overtones that echo
through its chapters. It is at the symbolic level that the locking
of the girl in the strong-room becomes part of the pattern of
Henry's repressed behaviour. It is at the same level that when
he has transferred to another legal firm, and after he has disas-
trously misunderstood the sudden appearance of two detectives,
his temporary collapse is seen as the inevitable result of a disturbed mental and emotional condition. The interior monologues
now take on more importance than ever before, becoming more
frequent and more frenzied. Fragments relating to his past life,
his basic feeling of insecurity, and his fear of physical incarcera-
tion mingle with his feelings of guilt and his dread of being cut
off by his respectable family. During a period of complete mental
and physical prostration, he is unable to work, to study, or even

to play tennis. He lies in bed and is looked after by his mother, who on one occasion, while taking his temperature, cries "Oh *Henry*" because of the bitten thermometer; and the interior monologue then takes possession of the theme:

> . . . *uncle Bob was hidden in the roses, but the grin on his face with petals stuck on all over it looked out, and a hand came out from lower down holding a glass of beer with the froth running over. And you held on to mother's hand and hid behind her skirt so that uncle Bob couldn't see you. Nothing could hurt you when you could run to mother or father. But uncle Bob was sitting in the back seat with Cherry on his knee, and he had Cherry's little red hat on instead of her, and the motor car was going down into the hole, and uncle Bob had his two arms round Cherry and the two of them were laughing and bouncing up and down, and you were saying isn't he naughty mother? Good riddance to bad rubbish. And the bell was ringing, and mother was kissing you goodbye, and you had to go, you had to, and all the time you were wanting to stay at home and look after her. But you had to sit in the motor car with Cherry and uncle Bob, and they were laughing but you were crying. Down, down, getting darker and darker, you were being shut in, covered over. And before you died you got the dirt in your eyes and you couldn't breathe. And in the dark you could hear Cherry and uncle Bob laughing and the sound of them kissing. Oh no no. And all you wanted was to stay with mother and look after her, and she'd look after you, snug as a bug in a rug, even if she had to get father to give you a hiding sometimes.*[20]

Unlike many novelists Sargeson is clearly not interested in following the slow process of a victim's recovery through the tortuous paths of psychiatric treatment. At no stage is his book a realistic account of the causes and development of a neurosis, but a series of glimpses into the mind of a child, growing through adolescence to early manhood. In order to overcome the difficulty of authorial involvement and explanation and to be able to reveal those domestic influences that primarily affected his protagonist he has been forced to adopt the method of indirect narration and depend on a disturbed interior monologue and traces of symbolism to give an impression rather than an exposition. The result is that at the realistic level the last episode of *When the Wind Blows* may be seen either as ridiculous or merely as

an inadequate version of a miraculous intervention that enables
Henry to take another look at life. It is convincing only at the
symbolic level. Through his window he sees his puritanical
father squatting down, nearly hidden behind a gooseberry bush
and looking towards the window of the room where his aunt
Clara is dressing. This startling repetition of the earlier scene in
which he himself had been the culprit causes a dramatically
unsatisfactory but symbolically amusing reversal in his whole
behaviour. The twelfth and final episode opens with Henry lying naked and alone on the grassy bank by a river, and as the
interior monologue takes over it is now for the first time calm
and reflective. Equilibrium of some kind has been restored or
achieved. He appears to have experienced a release from the
intolerable pressures that were destroying his personality. He
is free to criticize and meditate. He has at last untied the um-
bilical cord which attached him to his mother. No longer is he
oppressed by his own inadequacies, but his thoughts take him
back to scenes in which both his parents and aunt Clara had
played their parts, and these are punctuated by rueful and hu-
morous exclamations: poor mother, poor aunt Clara, poor father.
He is presumably ready to begin to discover his own identity,
to set out on his true pilgrimage through life. His last words
are: "I don't know a thing."

III *The Waiting World*

With what seemed to be a bland disregard for the normal requirements of plot sequence and psychological consistency,
Sargeson made little attempt at a smooth transition from *When
the Wind Blows* to the second part of *I Saw in My Dream*. He
was writing an experimental novel and it was moving to a
rhythm of his own devising. It was unlikely that it would be
immediately satisfying to anyone who could not make the necessary adjustments to his method of narration, and the little
critical appreciation the novel has received demonstrates that
few were prepared to make those adjustments. Nevertheless, a
careful examination of the text should make it apparent after a
time that early in the December, following Henry's partial recovery, he had answered an advertisement for a farm hand, and

had gone far away into the back country to live in a shack on
the dilapidated farm of "darky" Macgregor and his wife. David
Spencer, as he now calls himself, having adopted his own second
and his mother's maiden name, is scarcely recognizable as the
Henry Griffiths of the earlier part. He is highly regarded by the
Macgregors. He is a welcome guest of nearby farmers and is
warmly accepted by the Maoris, with whom he willingly drinks
beer. He seems genuinely horrified at the idea that he might
have attended Mission services in the city. He remembers it
was Gabriel Oak in *Far from the Madding Crowd* who was a
sheep shearer. He carries a copy of *The Winter's Tale* with him.
Henry, the pallid young victim of a suburban home, has completely disappeared, as though he were Antigonus pursued by a
bear and the sheep-shearing scenes were about to begin. His
whole being seems to have changed, or at any rate is in process
of change, and the carefully controlled method of narration does
not make it easier to identify him with the callow, repressed
and frantic Henry of *When the Wind Blows*. Down has come
baby and cradle and all. He is experiencing what amounts to a
rebirth, indicated by the italicized lines of the now less disturbing and less frequent interior monologue. He is lying "tightly
curled up in the chilly bed" and *why am I oh why am I here in
the cold and the dark? Cold bed rolling over to the sun, cold
embryo waiting to be born. Why am I waiamihea.*" [21] He has
become aware of what he does not know, and like the whole
countryside beyond the shack he is watching and waiting. In
imitation Maori he is asking a question that is material rather
than metaphysical. He is anxious to discover his relationship
with mankind and with the New Zealand scene that surrounds
him. His companion Johnny, ex-Borstal inmate and ex-seaman
from London, "had gone out into that waiting world, knowing
his relationship with it, perhaps not what you'd call conscious
of any such relationship, yet knowing it all the same." [22]

Superficially the novel now ceases to bear any marked resemblance to a series of disconnected episodes. It abandons the im-
pressionistic technique and becomes more orthodox, in the sense
that time is taken to develop slight incidents, to elaborate characters, to provide interludes and anecdotes that thicken its texture without destroying its unity, in order to show the pattern

of life and work in this sparsely populated community and the relationships between the human beings living there. The reader is not so entangled in the fragments of troubled consciousness of the hero. The background is more completely filled in, even if, according to Sargeson's method, this is effected by continual reference to Henry-Dave's perceptions and outlook. It is a background of hill country known to most New Zealanders; and working at the Macgregors or mustering sheep at the Andersons the young farm hand breathes in the familiar scents, sees the familiar sights, and experiences the familiar sensations of one to whom the outback life has become second nature. Like another pilgrim he has set forth on the road through the Slough of Despond to pass by the cave of PAGAN.

And while they stopped for their spells, breathing the close hot smells of grass and scrub and soil and sheep-dung, Dave would turn round and look back; and it was wonderful how different the valley looked once you were a bit higher up. It was beautiful. The tramline wound away down to the road, and the road down to the woolshed, and then on the pumice it turned white as it crossed down to the house with its red roof showing among the trees. And far away across the flat you could see the faint white line of the road that he and Johnny had come down, running at right angles. And it was all enclosed by the hills, green with new grass, brown with last year's fern, scarred by the slips, with a litter of fallen trees, dead, and blackened by fire; hills that were immense, yet from this distance their folds looked so smoothly and regularly finished that you somehow felt you *could* have been looking at something quite small—something that might have been only a model that you could hold on the palm of your hand.[23]

Soon the brief interior monologues, which now appear mainly when Johnny is talking and Henry-Dave's mind is elsewhere, are filled not with morbid memories and bewildered fantasies, but with a vivid sensational life. He marvels at the heat of the sun; he notices that because nesting time is almost past the birds are singing less; he is aware of unmoving patches of sunlight under a young magnolia tree; he recalls the hot and spicy smell in tea-tree scrub and the petals and the new seed cases *"a deep red, and divided up like jockey's caps"* with *"a thin plume coming out of their centre."* [24] He remembers

The moss that grew in humps was sphagnum. Florists would buy it.
And the creek was low since it was only showers a few days ago.
And clear, though it looked brown because the bed was brown, coated
with brown slime that under the water looked more like brown fur.
It had to thread among the logs, some of them enormous ones, that
had come down in the floods and got jammed, making pools. The
Maoris would come wading upstream, poking under the ledges with
sticks and tossing eels high up the bank. And carrying a billy for
koura. But the logs made it easy to cross, and every step you took
on the grass disturbed hopping and flying insects. And a fantail
came tumbling. You could hear its beak snapping only a foot or two
away.[25]

If a small aspect of the spirit of place is captured in this calm
reverie, other and wider aspects are rendered in terms of increasing concern with the sensuous abundance of the landscape.
It is a world of procreation, reproduction and fertility, a world
in which the frank conversation of the local inhabitants and the
rhythm of agricultural life can give Henry-Dave's thoughts release and a temporary resting-place. It is a world also in which
Maoris play an important, if dubious part; and for the first time
in his writing Sargeson attempts to examine some of the values
of a way of life that has little in common with the suburban respectability that was Henry's suffocating environment in *When
the Wind Blows*. At a Christmas party in Rangi's house, on the
gate to which was the scarcely decipherable word "Waiamihea,"
Henry-Dave sees the ancient Mrs. Parai:

You knew she was a woman, yet you told yourself you could hardly
have told from her face. Not that it was quite the face of a man
either—it was as though she was neither one sex nor the other. You
felt that she had lived so long she had become a new sort of human
being, something that you had never had any experience of. . . .
When she turned her eyes your way you felt it wouldn't have mat-
tered whether she had worn dark glasses or not. You'd still have
been looking into the blackest night, age-old and secret. And opaque.
These people were like that part of the valley outside that wasn't
lit by the moon—the bush side.[26]

This almost Lawrentian glimpse of hidden, mysterious, and
pagan otherness is not the prelude to sentimental rhapsodies on

the primitive. The Maoris are genuine Maoris; their failings and
their virtues belong to reality and not to myth and legend; but
their easy relationship with their traditional environment, their
free acceptance of the conditions of life, their kindness and their
rejection of the artificial conventions of European ways of living
have an attraction for Henry-Dave which is closely related to
the theme of the novel.

Beneath the surface story of small anecdotes, casual conversation and unspectacular happenings is a pattern of parallels and
contrasts which gives them meaning and significance and succeeds in achieving a precarious unity with *When the Wind
Blows.* No attempt is made to create a rural paradise or to go
outside the normal New Zealand setting except in relation to
the enigmatical figure of Cedric, the missing son of the Macgregors. As a character Cedric remains in the background. He
is neither a voice nor a presence, but as far as Henry-Dave is
concerned he is a powerful influence, a pilgrim who has gone before him and taken a road that leads either to the wilderness or
to more abundant life. He is central to the theme but he never
appears. He is a question mark from the time when Henry-Dave
comes to the Macgregors to the time when the *whare* and its two
inhabitants are buried beneath a sudden landslide. What has
happened to Cedric no one, unless his former playmate and
friend, the Maori Rangi, really knows and he will never tell.
Piece by piece Henry-Dave, and with him the reader, is able to
put together the story of Cedric's cave and of Cedric himself.
He seems to be on the edge of everyone's consciousness, whether,
as some think, he is working in a baker's shop in the city, or as
others maintain, his parents have had him certified, whether he
may still be living in a cave in the neighbourhood or whether
he has vanished from civilization altogether. The more he hears
of Cedric the more Henry-Dave feels in some peculiar way that
this young man may have found a solution to some of the problems with which he himself is beset.

Even as a small child Cedric had been strange and unman-
ageable. He was always disappearing to play and run around
naked like a wild thing with Rangi and the other Maori children.
By his actions he rejected both parental discipline and standardized education. He was a sprite of the bush country, a

willing outcast from civilization. And then as Henry-Dave learns from Johnny while the two of them are driving the sheep along the road to the saleyard, the Macgregors had conceived the horrible idea of shutting up Cedric for life, or at any rate for a long time, in a cave on the hillside behind the farm; but although Macgregor, and Johnny with him, had made the cave snug, and nearly completed a concrete wall around the opening, Cedric had disappeared before the plan could be carried out. When Henry-Dave expressed his horror of what had been the projected entombment of a living human being and of Johnny's acquiescent behaviour, the latter replied "they shut me up in that Borstal. So why shouldn't Cedric have been shut up if it would have taught him a good lesson?" [27] Then comes a line or two of interior monologue referring back to the strong-room of the law office in *When the Wind Blows: "wasn't he only trying to do his best for her, shutting her in there and locking the door, trying to make her into a good girl."* Cedric, however, had escaped into freedom, a freedom of his own; and only the Maori Rangi knew where he was or how he could be reached.

Escape or retreat? Which was it? How is a man to find freedom from the personal and social pressures to which he is continually subjected from the day he is born? These questions constitute the underlying theme of the whole book, and they have a distant parallel in the adventures of Huck Finn and that outcast's alliance with the Negro Jim against all the forces of so-called 'civilized society' that lead to conformity and the denial of the pagan virtues. As E. P. Dawson suggests: "Comparisons and contrasts between Mark Twain and Frank Sargeson, and the characters they create, press urgently for attention." [28] Nevertheless, Henry-Dave cannot forget his past, and when he is meditating on whether or not Cedric has found the answers to the questions that are always on the fringe of his consciousness he says:

> . . . *it's all right for Cedric. Cedric's Cedric. I'm pretty sure about that. But I'm not Dave, not exactly. And what does that mean? It means I'm what I was. Henry. But I'm also what I've become. Dave. Cedric never had a Henry to forget. Or TRY to forget. I have. I've been Henry, now I'm DAVE. But I'm only TRYING to be Dave.*

if it's question of place—I'm the wrong me. You have to be the right me in the right place. Like Cedric. The right place is the wrong place if you're the wrong me. And you have to BE the right me. Unless I could forget I could never change myself into the right me. And I couldn't, I know I couldn't. I'd remember. So for me, for MY me, it's not a question of place no it's a question of. It's. It's a question. A question of[29]

Henry-Dave knows that a solution to his predicament, the predicament of man, is not to be found either in retreat or escape, either in a return to the protective custody of the ball of contentment or in a flight to some refuge on the edge of civilization. When the whereabouts of Cedric's cave is being discussed at the Andersons' Christmas party, Ron Brackenfield, a sophisticated visitor from the city, slightly surprises the company by appearing in the living room naked except for a wreath of greenery dotted with red rosebuds "that sat askew on his head of Greek curls." [30] He immediately raises the conversation to a pseudo-intellectual level with "What about Plato's cave? What about the caves of (ahem) modern psychologists? . . . the shape of a ball—or a cave. Think of yourself inside—snug as a bug in a rug. Just as if you'd never been born." [31] We are back to the first page of *When the Wind Blows*.

I Saw in My Dream has a texture of correspondences and a complex design that emphasizes the contrasts without allowing them to dominate the narrative. The behaviour and conversation of the naked Brackenfield and the story of Cedric playing naked with a little Maori girl provide meanings that illuminate the return to the primitive. The account that Johnny gives of himself, combined with his twisted attitudes to morality and religion, lend support to Henry-Dave's reflection that *"He's like a glass you look in and see what you'd hoped you weren't any longer."* [32] The existence of a Little Bethel with its narrow doctrines in the remote countryside, the scarcely concealed contempt of the *pakeha* farmers and their wives for their dark-skinned associates, the antagonism between a New Zealand way of life and conventional English conduct, all indicate something that at one and the same time is related to a dramatization of the human scene and to an exploration of Henry-Dave's central problem of retreat, escape, or rebirth. Finally after the disastrous landslide which entombs the Macgregors in a sea of mud, he returns to his suburban home, having solved nothing that can be expressed in simple terms. At the end of *When the Wind Blows* he had discovered that he knew nothing. Now, as he watches his sister-in-law holding her baby above her head and smiling up at it with "Who loves you?" he knows that "Yes. He wanted to do something too. In his own way. Something special—*yes* YES." [33]

The structure of *I Saw in My Dream* is one that tends to obscure the major relevances to which most readers of novels are accustomed, and there will be many who find themselves in agreement with Lawrence Baigent's comment that it lacks "that unifying element—call it action, plot, drama, what you will—without which a novel cannot exist, if the term is to retain any meaning at all." [34] It may be observed, however, that except as a word vaguely descriptive of any extended narrative, the term has long since ceased to mean anything very precise or useful; and the pattern that has been indicated, neither underemphasized nor incoherent, provides exactly that unifying element without which critics hesitate to commend any imaginative work. Sargeson's conception of his theme is revealed clearly and unmistakably by threads of symbolism, by parallels and contrasts, by repetition of fragments of interior monologue. There is indeed too much pattern, rather than too little; but it is experimental and imperfectly absorbed into the surrounding texture. Interwoven with the narrative, it directs the reader to follow the progress of his hero towards the beginning of a search for personal identity and for fulfilment; but the interweaving requires close attention if the underlying pattern is to be adequately discerned. It demands a process of continual adjustment to the intentions and to the methods of the author. *I Saw in My Dream* cannot, therefore, be described as a triumphant success, but it is a considerable achievement, and as the same critic has commented: "Sargeson values his characters, his scenes, even such slight situations as arise, for their own sake . . . he succeeds brilliantly in conveying an exact sense of what it feels like to be in a certain place at a certain time." [35] As an experimental work containing many passages of translucent clarity his novel is one to which future readers are likely to turn in order to capture his vision of an important aspect of the New Zealand scene.

CHAPTER 6

One Set Apart

"Usually I feel I am some sort of victim."

I *New Departures*

IN a tailpiece to *The Puritan and the Waif* Sargeson was quoted as saying "There will be a great gap between *That Summer* and this new one after *I Saw in My Dream.* And yet, in the end one hopes it will all fit together as a whole." In other words he was aware in the Jamesian sense that there might be detected "a figure in the carpet" which would reveal not necessarily a philosophy of life nor an organic structure, for these terms are too pretentious, but a coherent attitude to the experience of living in New Zealand. At least he hoped that, however *I for One* might differ in technique and theme from his previous works, it would seem to be a continuation and an expansion of his earlier attempts to dramatize and evaluate significant areas of human behaviour.

When Helen Shaw adopted the title of *The Puritan and the Waif* for the symposium of critical essays on the work of Frank Sargeson, it was not chosen at random, nor without some insight into the nature of his writing and "the figure in the carpet"; but reviewing it in *Landfall* David Hall maintained that, because it was unable to include *I for One*, "a complete reassessment" [1] of Sargeson's work was now required. At first sight it is true that this short novel, very little shorter than *That Summer,* seemed to herald new departures in the writing of one for whom every beginning had been a new "raid on the inarticulate"; but, in fact, Sargeson had merely capitalized on his episodic manner and turned it to good advantage by adapting the rather outmoded diary form to his own purposes. His book became a record of a brief interlude in the life of a no longer young schoolteacher, Katherine Sheppard; and without straining the reader's credulity he was able to present the private thoughts of his heroine, Pamela-wise, as she communed with herself in the secrecy of her room, trying to clarify her own feelings after the events of the day.

Not only the form but the theme of *I for One* seemed to be a break with the past. *That Summer* had been a series of episodes concerned with a fringe character on the edge of civilization who had no wish to partake in the business and social activities of the majority. It was also a love story in which he sought relief for his pent-up feelings and his hunger for comradeship, while he rejected the habits of life which had followed an alliance between a decaying puritanism and the gospel of worldly success. *I Saw in My Dream* had been concerned with the emotional and mental starvation of a human being who, threatened with life-long imprisonment within the narrow circle of middle-class imperatives, was able to resist both flight and retreat. *I for One* is a love story seen from the woman's point of view. It reveals, therefore, some of the less obvious consequences of a sheltered existence, of an instinctive withdrawal from society, of a subjection to and an acceptance of moral attitudes which she has had no opportunity to test. Indirectly, Sargeson was still preoccupied with the puritan and the waif.

The mask that Sargeson found was the most difficult he had yet attempted to wear. Although he was accustomed to the art of speaking through the mouths of many and varied characters, he had never before tried to speak for any length of time in the person of a young woman, particularly in the person of a young woman of refinement and conventional respectability. Once again he had chosen to silence the voice of the author and place his central character in immediate relation with the reader. This meant that the story must be completely self-contained, and not only the story, but the memories, the background, and the whole complicated process of human development. Any observation about his heroine's past life must come easily and naturally from her reflections on the present situation. Any casual comment must carry a relevance to the story unfolded, and a meaning to the reader. This poses an enormous strain on the writer; and the best tribute that can be paid to Sargeson's handling of his theme

and his identification with his character is that never for a
moment does the author's voice become audible, and never for
a moment does the imaginary diarist lose control of her idiom
or become inept in her account of reveries and feelings. She
does but slenderly know herself and finds it difficult to describe,
even for her own satisfaction, her motives and her moods, and
yet her hesitations are few and her impulses many. She becomes
the most fully alive and the most complex character that Sargeson had tried to create, alive in her uncertainty as in her inability
to plumb the depth of her own nature. "I seem to be—doodling!"
Katherine confides to her diary, "It happens I suppose when one
is drained out and exhausted, and one's thoughts are idling.
It is on such occasions that one remembers about the still small
voice, and who knows?—perhaps it speaks to us through the
language of our doodlings. But alas, I'm afraid it is a language
which I for one aren't clever enough to decipher." [2] "I for one,"
the title, is an indication of the heroine's lack of self-knowledge.

Katherine Sheppard is not clever. She is an ordinary teacher
in a girls' school, not yet of middle age, but conscious of her
increasing years and her state of virginity. She has no marked
interests beyond her pupils, the reading of thrillers, and scrib-
bling at intervals in the exercise books she calls her diary. She
is a young woman to whom nothing seems to happen or, indeed,
has happened except her school-girl passion for her friend Unice,
to whom her thoughts continually recur, and what she had imagined might have turned into a quiet love affair with a young
consumptive. She has always been protected by her parents, not
only from the blows but from the complexities of life. She has
been brought up to observe the proprieties of the moderately
well-to-do, and has been restricted to the family triangle except
for the occasional party at which she has always felt an outsider.
Although she vaguely suspected that things happened of which
she had no conception, she had never known what went on.
"Sometimes," she confesses, "I've wished that behaviour could
have been really and truly unrestrained. Because if I'm to find
myself excluded, I'd much rather it was from the real thing instead of something merely ambiguous. But *why* am I excluded?" [3]
It is only at this late date, after making entries in her diary over
a period of three months that she feels, mistakenly, that she has

encountered the world, the mysterious world where things happen and people let themselves go. She has become aware not only that she has never really known herself, but that she has not known even her father or her mother in any intimate way, much less has she an inkling of what their marriage might have meant to them. She is accustomed to and approves of the family reticence; and it is only in the pages of her diary that she admits to herself that she feels like Jephthah's daughter, the biblical character whose name she had forgotten "who went out among the hills and bewailed her virginity." [4] Then, looking towards her bedroom window, outside which a gale is raging, she is thankful that "one should be protected against such ravishing fury by so frail a barrier";[5] and one is aware that Sargeson is using language to reveal more than his character knows. In her daydreams she is never the heroine: "It would be difficult to say my role exactly, but usually I feel I am some sort of victim. I can't think why." [6]

Slowly and adroitly, without sacrificing too much of the realism associated with the diary form and the nuances of speech suitable to such a limited character, Sargeson establishes Katherine Sheppard in her setting of small activities and introverted behaviour. It is not surprising that she is afflicted by severe attacks of migraine, nor that she constantly accuses herself of minor moods of petulance and suffers from fits of depression. She wishes to have a home of her own "and stay there forever, contented always to attend to all the little tasks that have to be done without ever wanting to put one's foot on the street outside." [7] It would be a refuge from an inexplicable world, a cave of retreat from disturbing contact with human experience. Her attitudes remind her friend Hubert Nock, an American psychologist, with whom she has the brief and abortive love affair which provides her diary with its main theme, of the women of Nantucket whose religious background was such that the usual pleasures were denied them and who had recourse to a daily dose of opium in order to make life more tolerable and to compensate them for so many emotional restraints. The thrillers that she reads, like the tales to which Frances was addicted in Sargeson's short story *In the Midst of Life,* are a substitute for the opium of the Nantucket women. All these small details about

Katherine Sheppard are slipped in so naturally and unobtru-
sively that the reader becomes aware of their significance only
within the framework of the whole narrative. Her diary becomes
much more than a medium for feminine prattle or a record of a
sentimental attachment. It becomes a densely organized pattern
of references and cross-references which succeeds in illuminating
her personality without forsaking what could have been her
normal mode of expression. She is a character whom it is difficult
to like and more difficult to admire because of her abysmal
ignorance and her neurotic impulses. Yet such is her naivety,
her longing for candour and sincerity in her own conduct and
that of her friends, that like Emma in Jane Austen's novel she
claims the reader's affection and commands sympathy even
though he may be repelled by her self-centredness, her capacity
for being shocked and her inability to understand herself or
others. Sargeson has managed to create out of very unpromising
material a portrait of a living human being. He has interwoven
so many ironies that the pathetic and rather ridiculous love affair
becomes the tragedy of an unfulfilled and inhibited heroine.

Even the fragments of description, referring to the progress
of the seasons from June to October, which mark the limits of
the diary, carry with them indications of a wistfulness and charm,
as well as an undertone of a deeper meaning, that lift his narrative to a level of significance hardly equalled elsewhere in his
writing. Katherine's final entry in her diary is:

It seems I hardly noticed, but during the past few weeks spring has
come and vanished—and today really come again. I have been out
in the garden once, and must get out again. The sun shines from
a clear sky, and the light on leaves and flowers is a marvel, the air
is warm yet fresh and fragrant—and so still that even now I can
hear the bees in their thousands, competing with the little white-eyes
for the honey of our flowering acacia. I can hear the starlings walking on the roof above my head, and when I drew my blind this
morning I saw a thrush flying with straws in its beak, looking almost
as though it had grown cat's whiskers. But I don't know why I
should seem to see all these things with the eyes of a stranger, of
one set apart.[8]

The first and last sentences of this passage are carefully arranged,
so that in the simplest possible way what is conveyed is not

merely a description of the onset of spring, but one of a brief interlude in the story of a woman who through the pressures of time, upbringing, and social environment has remained a stranger to life, has remained one set apart.

From the moment when soon after her father's death the entries in the diary begin, it becomes apparent that Katherine has never had a chance to commence to live. Her horizon has been bounded by the figure of her father, by her admiration for his goodness, his generosity, his kindness towards herself and by her sympathy with his dimly recognized loneliness. He too has been one set apart, and she has no knowledge at all of his earlier more exciting and unrestrained life. "For me, ever since I can remember, father has been the very image of those trustworthy characteristics that seem so very desirable in a man," [9] she records primly; and as she examines her state of mind after meeting Hubert Nock she discovers "he is mature, so fully adult and reliable that I can't help being reminded of father." [10] Sargeson's method of presenting his story through the private scribblings of his heroine prevents him from over-emphasizing her unacknowledged search for a father figure. No more than in *When the Wind Blows* was he attempting to write anything in the nature of a psychology case history. He was concerned with delineating some of those features in the New Zealand scene which from his own observation and in his opinion had helped to create the half-men and half-women who were trying to live their incomplete lives by ignoring whole areas of human experience. If he chose to take a special instance, suitably dramatized in terms of the novel he was writing, this did not destroy the validity of what may be called his argument—that the freedom to grow into, to reach towards, a full and richly sensitive life is checked by social and domestic pressures that have little relation to real living.

II   *The Eyes of a Stranger*

What his medium allowed him to do he did. Near the beginning of Katherine's diary, and separated by four days, are two small episodes which help to cast an oblique light on the writer herself. Soon after her father's death, when old Mrs. Sheppard was unable to get up one morning, Katherine discovered what she described as a "shocking" thing. Her mother was lying on the very edge of the double bed and resisted all her daughter's attempts to persuade her to lie in a more normal position with the words "*You* don't understand, Katherine. . . . I never could bear to be any closer to that man." [11] A few days later, when Katherine called on her friend Else and failed to find her at home she was invited into the next door house by an eccentric old spinster. This Miss Drake lived with a married sister who was separated from her husband, and the first enquiry that she made of Katherine was to ask whether she was a Miss or a Mrs., seeming to be inordinately pleased to learn that she was the former. "It's you and me who are the lucky ones dear—only *they* don't know," [12] was the last remark the spinster made as they bade each other goodbye; and these words struck Katherine as being peculiarly revolting. Both her shock at her discovery of something inexplicable in her mother's marriage and her revulsion from Miss Drake's crazy observation are symptoms of her ignorance of life and her desire for a normal sexual relationship which, even at her age, she cannot fully comprehend. Another occasion when her reaction to an incident is complicated by an exaggerated consciousness of her vulnerable virginity concerns two adolescent girls. They had followed her on one of her solitary beach walks and had finally dropped an obscene note in her path. She was not so much shocked as horrified that she had been chosen as the object of their disgusting practical joke. Her horror was personal rather than moral. Her sense of being always a victim seemed fully justified.

These few examples illustrate the way in which *I for One* should be regarded as an episodic novel of a different kind from *That Summer*, in that the structure of episodes is fully accounted for by the diarist's technique, which follows a chronological order but is able to arrange telling situations at the author's will. Many of them are most memorable, for Sargeson can always present in a vivid and dramatic manner a small vignette which is effective because of its clarity and detail. Each succeeds in adding to the portrait of Katherine, who is discovered to be strangely lacking in those qualities which usually attract men or would indicate an ability to face life with confidence and understanding. She is unable to love as a woman should love. She is sensitive in her relation with children, as the incident of Katie's drawings amply demonstrates, but even here it indicates more precisely Katherine's extreme sensitivity to her increasing years and her desire to seem as youthful as ever to her little pupils. She is sensitive in her relation with her mother, though hindered in her reactions by a lack of penetration that amounts almost to a constitutional disease. She is eager to sympathize, to be maternal and compassionate, but she is unable to love.

The story of her earlier relationship with Colin, the young consumptive whom she had visited regularly in hospital (and significantly enough she repeats this practice with Dr. Nock), is one that is as pathetic as it is absurd. She overpowers him with kindness. She fusses. She looks after him; and she never knows why he is so careful not to commit himself in any way or respond to her devotion, even if she is humiliated to hear from this mother's boy (and once again Hubert Nock's mother in distant America looms large in that psychologist's mind) "that I couldn't be doing more for him in his illness if I had been his own mother." [13] Her friendship with Hubert Nock begins in much the same manner, as, in one of her rare flashes of insight, she almost recognizes, for "*never* are my tenderest feelings aroused so much as when I am attracted by somebody who deserves compassion." [14] She alternates between sympathy and gentle bossiness, between the approach of a magazine reader to the strong, handsome male and an unrelenting search for a 'Mr. Right' who will be both father figure and child-man; but she can never give herself completely. She has no acquaintance with physical passion, and mental passion is quite beyond her scope.

The situation in which she finds herself with Hubert Nock is one that would have made even a school girl suspect her own behaviour and motives as well as those of her supposed lover. Because we see the latter only through Katherine's eyes he remains a hazy if essential character in the background of the novel; and, as Katherine does not listen to much of what he says, but indulges in mental "doodling," he is more enigmatical than necessary. She herself admits that the story, seen from his point of view, might have been very different. It would be wrong

to say that all her defenses crumble the moment she meets him
at Else's party, because her sense of propriety is too fixed, her
conviction of her mother's respectable standards is too firm, her
lack of anything that could be called passion for Hubert Nock
is too obvious, her determination, like Pamela's, that she must
have authentic marriage lines to show to her dear parent is too
strong, and her fear of losing her virginity too tremulous for
her to be swept away by the expression of a love that is neither
violent nor irresistible.

Controlled by his method, by his characters as well as by
inclination, Sargeson avoids any sultry dramatization of passionate love-making. By preference, he renders what goes on in
Katherine's mind and how her feelings are affected. The truth
is that not very much that is coherent goes on in her mind, and
her feelings are so tangled that she cannot confide them very
clearly even to her diary. Her early years of sheltered seclusion
have prepared her for the role of victim and not for that of
thinker or participator in life. It is the movement of the language
more than the content of her sentences that reveals the process
of her thought. Her mental 'doodling' is paralleled by Hubert's
habit of wandering on and on, evidently unperturbed by the
inattention of his listener; and for all his manly exterior, his
verbosity, and his apparent sophistication, he is hardly more in
control of his thoughts and actions than is Katherine. The result
is that each of the episodes in which they are involved becomes
slightly unreal because it seems to be a meeting between two
vacuous and disarranged minds. Furthermore, the reader is
vaguely troubled by the fact that the subject of marriage was
broached only about five weeks after they had first met at Else's
party. During that period Hubert had been in hospital for a
fortnight, and although Katherine had paid him daily visits
after school for half that time, it was when they first went out
together to the Jolly Sailor that she was left with an important
question she must answer. Her method of dealing with this
question is a further indication of her distorted outlook on life:

   Dilemma. The word has been so constantly in my mind that I have
looked it up in father's big Dictionary. . . . It is amusing to think
that a dilemma has two horns, but quite horrifying if you have to

decide which one to impale yourself on. They are both evils, so I am informed, and equal ones. It is, alas, my own situation exactly! And yet, how strange that I should feel so light-hearted this morning. Can it be that I am already resigned? After all, if one must choose, with only bad things to choose from! Or is it because the morning is so mild and lovely. When I looked out first thing, I saw that the buds on the pussy willow were just about to break. So another spring is just around the corner, and it's a poor heart—as folks say. But if only we could be like the seasons, and have our lives without any choosing among good things and bad.[15]

Of course her migraine returned more severely. She had very recently been surprised and horrified by her mother, who of all people had drawn her attention to a risqué joke in the book she was reading. She was upset by having to make the momentous decision between two evils—her maiden state and union with Hubert; and once she had decided to say "Yes" she forthwith began to lament her virginity and to think of marriage as a kind of death. This was no whirlwind courtship, no ardent anticipation of the linking of bodies and minds, but a rather fearful and bewildering process in which doubt and uncertainty played their confusing parts. In her daydreams she looked at the ranges from a corner of the garden; her whole nature seemed to respond to their fancied beckoning; and she yearned for "a larger share in such a perfect day." [16] A little later, on the way to the Museum, she was fascinated by a radiant girl who looked like one of the Muses; but inside the building the sight of the great carved war canoe for some reason reminded her that she would never be able to dream her way out of her present life. Her hold on reality is tenuous. Even on her second meeting with Hubert, when she was worried by what she believed was his misunderstanding of her affirmative answer on the telephone, she wrote afterwards in her diary:

I . . . became so wrapped up in my thoughts about what he had already said, that I listened with only half an ear, until our taxi stopped at the Jolly Sailor and I realized to my astonishment that Hubert was talking about getting married. I could have exclaimed Who! When! How!—or something equally absurd, but he was paying for the taxi, and then he swept me inside the place at such a

rate I was quite breathless by the time we reached our table. . . .
and *now*, I must confess, I listened with every bit of ear that I
possess.

Oh yes, it was all quite amazing to listen to. Now, instead of
feeling that I wasn't there, I felt more as though I just didn't exist
at all. Not as I know myself. Hubert had me taped, as the saying
is, all measured up and suitably cut and shaped to fit into his plans
for our future together.[17]

Katherine thought him "unbelievably *solemn*" and became so
immersed in introspection that once again she ceased to listen
and began to experience "indescribable feeltings of doubt and
confidence."

This treatment of the business of courtship and marriage
would be a serious defect in the novel if Sargeson were writing
the love story of two more or less normal people. However, he
is far more interested in the minds and attitudes of those whose
reactions to events are conditioned by their own lives of un-
reality. He is interested in the victims, in those who live apart,
in men and women who are imperfectly adjusted to the ortho-
doxy of repression. The world of daydreams in which Katherine
lives is an unreal world. Her ideas of people, of her closest
relatives, even of herself have been distorted because she has
never been able, never been allowed, to know the facts on
which valid conclusions could be based. She has been enclosed
by a wall of silence and has picked up her slender knowledge
of the world as best she could. Longing for candour and tidiness
in her dealings with people she has been surrounded by deceit,
misnamed 'reticence,' so that when a fortnight later Hubert con-
fessed that he already had a wife she was thrown into fresh
disorder.

Her lover's account of his early and quixotic marriage with
a refugee Jewish girl, abandoned in Paris by an American newspaper man and who had been immediately abandoned by himself is not calculated to create confidence even in the infatuated
and naive Katherine. She, however, is very ready to sympathize
with his youthful folly, but is puzzled by his self-congratulation
on not deceiving her, while at the same time continuing to
persuade her to go through the form of marriage with him. His
reason for not wishing to take the necessary steps to free him-

self from his legal wife, who after accepting money for some years had ceased all communication, is that his mother, like himself, has ideals, and he is one of them. She would almost certainly learn his secret and be upset. Psychologist though he is, he lives in a world in which clarity of thought and attitude has little place. Both Hubert and Katherine are sentimentalists, in the sense that they mistake the shadow for the reality. Because their lives have been encompassed by deception they are incapable of looking steadily at any object or idea. They have succumbed to social and personal pressures which they do not pretend to understand. Their argument, if such it can be called, turns into a foggy debate in which neither can have the victory, because neither is clear about motives or intentions:

I couldn't help saying how very much tied to his mother's apron strings he seemed to be, and he replied that if he was, then wasn't it up to me to help him free himself. And instead of helping I was arguing and raising objections. And it was a disappointment, because when he first met me he had thought he had at last met a woman who wouldn't try to boss everybody in sight. And anyhow, wasn't I tied to my own mother's apron strings? Or worse, wasn't I tying myself of my own free will? There was only one rule for people tied up in these situations, and it was all in the proverb, What the eye doesn't see, the heart doesn't grieve over . . . Why did I want to bring the dead past alive again? What could be the good? He said it made him think of the dead people in the cemetery coming out of their graves and turning up in their homes again. What heartbreaks there would be! Thank God it could never happen, but wasn't I trying to make something like it happen? And what for? For the sake of the conventions, just so that I could be doing the right thing. Was I as socially-minded as all that? The thing that was socially right could be the wrong thing from the human standpoint. And the socially wrong thing could be the morally good thing.[18]

There can be no end to an argument of this kind. The only considerations that are omitted are human motives, self-understanding and passion.

III *A Sheltered Existence*

It would be a great mistake, here as elsewhere, to imagine that Sargeson should be identified with either of the protagon-

ists. As always, he is wearing a mask, a series of masks. He is
revealing how people talk, how they deceive themselves, how
they convince themselves, when all the time their thinking is
largely determined by social and psychological pressures, and
their craving for sympathy and love. Although the plot structure
of *I for One* is much more taut than usual with Sargeson, it is
only the means whereby human behaviour can be examined.
Although the characters, and particularly Katherine, are more
individual and more firmly established than in any of his writings
except *That Summer,* they are neither an end in themselves nor
the sole object of Sargeson's endeavour. He is by no means a
character-monger. His aim is to uncover the springs of human
conduct, to explore, in puritan and in waif, in the confused and
the inarticulate, those aspects that cast reflections on the society
around them, a society in which deceit abounds and an artificial reticence takes its human toll. The narrative is the means
whereby social and personal values can be examined. Yet, *I for
One* has a distant resemblance to the rather slick and melo-
dramatic magazine story that depends for its interest on the
swift manipulation of event and an ingenious but contrived
pattern of human relationships. The twists and turns of the plot
and the series of surprising discoveries made by Katherine tend
to dull the reader's critical instinct. They offer a form of excitement which diverts attention from the predicament of one whose
experience of life has been minimal.

Nevertheless, Katherine's discoveries are basic plot material
because her mother's dilemma in relation to her father provides
a contrast to and an ironic commentary on her own experiences
with Hubert Nock. They are closely related to her incapacity to
face the realities of life and, most important of all, they give
the author opportunities for exploring the inhibitory consequences of a deceitfully "respectable" approach to female development. It is at this level that *I for One* ceases to be contrived
and fanciful and becomes a novel of some power and significance.

Katherine's series of discoveries began with her mother's cry
"You don't understand . . . I never could bear to be any closer
to that man." They continued through a number of small reve-
lations until, suffering from nervous prostration, she found to
her horror that it had been calmly and erroneously concluded

that she had had an abortion. Her mother spoke to her "as one wrong doer to another" [19] and Katherine was unable to stop her "because how unpleasant for mother to hear the innocent truth about myself, when what she had said had told me so much about *her.*" [20]

But before telling me what I should have been told years ago, mother began by saying, she hoped everything was right with me now. It was such a dangerous thing to have done, particularly at the hands of anybody so lacking in experience as that young girl must be. And she did hope I understood that it was against the law and must not be talked about. I could trust her of course, but I should be very careful about trusting any of my friends. I mustn't think that she was blaming me, she went on, because if anybody was to blame it was herself. When she was young her own mother had kept her in ignorance, but luckily she had had her wits about her and learned for herself. But it was a mistake to think that everybody learned for themselves. [21]

Katherine's ignorance even of her own family and, because of the blanket of silence that surrounded her, of herself and the world in relation to herself was so complete that the boundaries of her life had never been enlarged until her father's death and her association with Hubert. Later entries in her diary concern her fortuitous meeting with Hilda James, who proved to be her step-sister, and her discovery that the beautiful girl she had seen at the Museum was Hilda's daughter. Her suspicion and then the certainty that her mother was capable of prying into her private thoughts and affairs by reading pages of her precious diary made her doubt human integrity, and when her mother cleverly evaded any discussion about Hilda James and therefore of her own or her husband's married life, Katherine was made aware that her sheltered existence had been based on illusion and the suppression of truth.

After she had committed the "folly" of trying to see Hubert at his hotel and instead of him had encountered Hilda James and her daughter in the lounge, after she had gone on "the last ride together" with Hubert and he had tried to explain that everything had been a big mistake, she once again indulged in the further "folly" of trying to see him in order to patch up

their shattered relations. It is then, when for the second time
she finds Hilda and her daughter Helen in the hotel lounge
with Hubert that "the wonderful child," her father's grand-
daughter, begins to play her comparatively silent but important
role in the novel. Brief though it is, it is sufficient to indicate
that Sargeson's sympathetic imagination is not confined to the
portrayal of people to whom the depression of the early thirties
was a living reality. As in some of his later short stories, notably
Just Trespassing, Thanks, which in 1965 won the Katherine
Mansfield award, he shows that the "beat" generation is not
beyond the scope of his art. Helen is what her brittle and shallow
mother calls "modern." She sees through parental shams and
pretensions. She is intelligent and can spend hours reading *Moby
Dick* in preference to thrillers; but she is conversant with radio
serials and can discuss them with Katherine's mother. She can
be unmannerly and off-hand, but is quick to see and comprehend
the situation in which the emotionally distraught Katherine finds
herself. She has surprising tact and penetration that without
being cynical is clear-sighted. She is everything that Katherine
is not; and so she not only steers her much older "aunt" through
the most embarrassing and pathetic episode of her life, but since
her mother and Hubert are leaving to be married she insists
on accompanying Katherine home and staying with her for a
week. The short glimpses of Helen seen through the pages of
the diary give a radiance to the conclusion of *I for One* that is
as unexpected as it is ironic, for the "wonderful child," in
Katherine's words, is adjusted to the modern world in a way
that the older woman can never hope to be. She has rebelled
early enough to avoid the cramping effects of repression. She
has not mistaken shadows for reality, nor allowed daydreams
and illusions to hide the truth from her. She has been able to
accept life with open integrity and although, as her mother
complains, she does not seem to know the difference between
right and wrong, she knows the difference between good and
evil, as she herself with a sidelong glance at Graham Greene's
Brighton Rock asserts.

I for One is a disturbing novel, because, although it has a
well-defined plot and an impressive structure, it leaves so many
gaps in an argument concerned with conventional behaviour and

the reticence of a moderately well-to-do household. It is disturbing also because Katherine's involvement with her lover and the revelation of the way in which Mrs. Sheppard had "lived in sin" with Katherine's father must be regarded as too much of a special case for the general conclusions that seem to stem from the patterned plot. It is doubtful that the human symbols are so adequate that they can be said to illuminate the whole social scene. Nevertheless, Sargeson has been prepared to sacrifice a specious form of realism in order to dramatize the consequences for human behaviour of female subservience to the requirements of "respectability." He has paid the reader the compliment of assuming that he is willing and able to watch the ironies develop and interlock as the reflections of the heroine are confided to her diary and as the series of events and discoveries unfold. Katherine seems to have learnt little for herself. She remains a stranger to the world and as one set apart. She had said of the language of her doodlings "I'm afraid it is a language which I for one aren't clever enough to decipher." It is left to the reader to decipher the language that defeated Katherine; the occupation can be both fascinating and rewarding.

CHAPTER 7

Past and Future

"My business is to create."

WILLIAM BLAKE

I *Dramatic Experiments*

FROM the early years of his career as a writer, Sargeson had been concerned with new beginnings and with new directions. By New Zealand standards he was an innovator and an originator. He was becoming part of a tradition which he himself had helped to create. He had experimented with language and had sought to adapt and devise forms for material which seemed to him most in need of dramatization. Nevertheless, he had been animated by no desire to appear original nor to indulge in a purely formal art of expression. If he was determinedly provincial in execution, he was not parochial in outlook.

After almost thirty years of dedicated craftsmanship, he had produced only a slender body of work, which did not gain by the peculiar difficulties and frustrations that confronted a pioneer New Zealand writer. He was still occupied with short stories written in his own idiom and revealing increased subtlety and skill. He had published two short novels that could not easily be fitted into any of the established literary categories. He had written a full-length novel, the three sections of which were stamped with his own characteristic signature, and explored aspects of New Zealand life which had never before been fully examined. Then, in the late fifties, he turned his attention to drama.

It might appear strange that Sargeson had apparently rejected a form of writing that depended greatly on the spoken voice, with which he had been experimenting for so long in fiction. Certainly his interest in dramatic literature was of no recent origin, for in the early thirties, during the last stages of the

Depression, when he was registered as unemployed and working on relief and at various casual jobs, he turned his unpublished novel "Blind Alleys" into a three-act play and wrote another three-act play, "Secret Places," both of which still remain among his unpublished works. A little later he had shown his interest in dramatic productions by writing occasional articles for *Tomorrow* on such themes as "The People's Theatre," "T.S. Eliot in Auckland," and "The Insect Play"; and in his commentary on the Auckland production of Capek's drama he had said:

I suppose I'm prejudiced against this play because it doesn't happen to be in my line. It's the spoken word that attracts me most in plays, the spoken word combined with such lively and passionate realism that the whole thing becomes symbol. Karel Capek's interested in symbol too, but in this play he tries to get it out of fantasy instead of realism, and that just doesn't happen to be in my line.[1]

Speaking of the production he said: "I don't go to the theatre to see shop-window displays by Milne and Choyce," [2] and writing of Eliot's *Murder in the Cathedral* he affirmed that "it is necessary for a dramatic statement to be both verbal and demonstrative." [3]

These observations suggest that Sargeson was working out for himself certain principles of dramatic production to which later he would try to remain faithful—a play depended on its language, on the reality and expressiveness of its utterance; it depended not on elaborate settings nor on fantasy, but on a realistic portrayal of life so vigorously presented that it transcended the immediate and local events described. He was still devoted to a concept of imaginative realism which was implied in those lines from Conrad to which he frequently returned: "What I am trying to achieve by the power of the written word is to make you hear, to make you feel—it is, above all, to make you *see*. That and no more, and it is everything." It was not only the written word, however, but the spoken word that had always received his attention in the short stories he had written, the spoken word uttered by some person who had become alive and vocal in the mask that Sargeson was wearing for the occasion. In his reminiscences of his introduction to the plays of

Shakespeare he recalled the lines beginning "Death that hath
sucked the honey of thy breath . . ." spoken by a young actor
in the Alan Wilkie Shakespearean tour of New Zealand, and
wrote:

It was as though that young man had wiped a window clean with
his words—providing me with a view which, previously obscure, was
now seen to be radiantly clear. Also, it was a double view—or rather
I should say it was a view I could on the one hand comprehend as a
positive invitation to enter the enchanted landscape of the poet's
imagination; and on the other as a complete denial of every confident
and complacent assertion to which, as a New Zealander, I was so
very much accustomed. But above all, I returned that night to my
lodgings drunk with the understanding that the totality of splendour
which attached to the world of Shakespeare's imagination was inseparably rooted in *words:* it was an infinite comfort to know that I
could be separated from it only by being separated from the printed
page. Nor have I since wavered in my belief that Shakespeare's
primary attraction, and indeed his primary value, resides in the range
and variety of his verbal images and their incomparable splendour.[4]

Such a passage as this again emphasizes, as his writing had
always made manifest, that it was the word itself, spoken or
written, to which Sargeson had been so strongly attracted, not
the word alone, but as an indication of thought and meaning.
It also suggests that the environment in which he lived was not
one conducive to dramatic art. There was no tradition of the
theatre in New Zealand. Shakespeare's plays might be a part of
the educational establishment, second only to the Bible; but
there were few performances of these or any other plays, except
for the activities of sometimes lively but more often inferior
groups of amateurs. Sargeson records what many New Zealanders
would be able to endorse from their own experience, that in
London he had indulged himself with an orgy of theatre-going.
He was "fascinated by the technique of acting and speech for
the stage" and "frequented evenings run by a Compton Street
group known as Playroom Six, where the skilful work of players
who were unemployed could be observed at very close quarters." [5]
In New Zealand, however, just as there was no theatrical

tradition of any importance, and companies of overseas actors made only very occasional appearances, so, and as a necessary consequence, there were very few plays written and fewer still published. Their paucity is revealed by E.H. McCormick's *New Zealand Literature* (1959) which refers in passing to only three or four of any slight significance, and these were almost the byproducts of writers whose medium was verse. The well-known poet R.A.K. Mason had published in 1938 a short radio play *Squire Speaks,* English both in tone and in literary origins, and followed it some years later with a brief script for a dance drama called *China.* Before Charles Brasch had returned to New Zealand, founded *Landfall,* and published several volumes of verse, he had produced *The Quest,* being words for a mime play; and D'Arcy Cresswell, likewise in England, had been at work for twelve years on his poetic drama, *The Forest,* which was eventually published in 1952 and not performed until 1963. Finally, and perhaps more striking in its impact on those who were watching and waiting for a native drama, the poet Allen Curnow had produced *The Axe* in 1948. Otherwise there were very few dramatic experiments apart from the earlier work of Bruce Mason and Claude Evans until the late fifties.

It was not until 1960 that a reviewer of James K. Baxter's two plays, then recently performed in Wellington, was prompted to refer rather optimistically to "a strong new impulse" [6] in New Zealand drama which seemed to parallel the upsurge in the production of novels. Nevertheless, there is little evidence to suggest that a theatrical tradition is even in process of being evolved, much less a tradition that is concerned with native drama. There are some stirrings among theatre lovers for the creation of a National Theatre, but as late as 1963 a commentator in *Landfall* was saying "the movement to encourage the writing of New Zealand plays has not so far been conspicuously successful." [7] By that time, it is true, not only had Sargeson's two plays, "A Time for Sowing" and "The Cradle and the Egg," been performed, but Bruce Mason, Stella Jones, James K. Baxter, Allen Curnow, and Claude Evans had shown some of the possibilities of an indigenous drama. Once again Sargeson had become a co-pioneer in dramatic endeavours, and had written and collaborated in producing two plays which, whatever their permanent value, may be regarded as continuations of his work as experimenter and stimulator.

In "Writing a Novel" he had concluded his radio talk with a few brief sentences on the possibilities of historical exercises in that genre.

So far the time has not been ripe for the historical novel in New Zealand. So far we have been too much tied to the event to think of an imaginative interpretation of the event. There have been too many old timers about only too ready to trip up the novelist on points of detail. Eventually it seems to me the detail does not matter a very great deal, or at any rate only in as much as it will stimulate the novelist's imagination. Of course, he will need many resources besides an imagination capable of responding to the right stimulus, but if the right time has not arrived yet, then I suggest it may not be very far off, and in any case one must always accept the honest and sometimes very interesting attempts that have already been made at imaginative interpretation.

When these words were written Sargeson was not immediately contemplating any elaborate successor to William Satchell's *The Greenstone Door*. He was not interested in reconstructing a panoramic picture of early New Zealand or in writing a prose saga of several generations of New Zealand families. As in his previous works he was still fascinated by a conflict involving a process of adjustment or nonadjustment to ways of life that clashed with the human aspirations of a bewildered and complex personality; and before long he was deeply immersed in an attempt to recreate an imagined episode in the life of the much maligned and self-tortured Thomas Kendall, that strange Church of England missionary who had come to the Bay of Islands in 1814.

II   *A Time for Sowing*

Kendall, devout Christian, amateur anthropologist, writer of the first Maori primer, whose scandalous conduct had led to his withdrawal by the Church Missionary Society only eight years after his arrival, has become, together with the incredible Baron de Thierry, one of the very few historical figures whose lives have become legend and have attracted the attention of biographer, historian, novelist, and poet alike. R.M. Burdon's brief account in *New Zealand Notables, Series 3* (1950), and Keith Sinclair's poem "Memorial to a Missionary" in his slim volume *Songs for a Summer* (1952) are two of the more permanent results of Kendall's dubious pilgrimage in New Zealand. Other results are written in the whole story of Maroi-Pakeha relations and in what Sinclair calls "the legacy of guilt" which to a greater or less extent we all inherit.

It was a sentence in Burdon's biography that, according to one of Sargeson's letters, first stimulated him to write about Kendall, and he acknowledged his debt in the published version of *A Time for Sowing*. A minor and more personal cause was that Sargeson's maternal grandfather had come from the fen country in Lincolnshire, and he still had a relative living close to North Thoresby where the disgraced missionary had been born in 1778. A far more powerful reason for his attraction to Kendall was the spiritual and domestic dilemma in which the latter found himself in New Zealand. He was torn between his zeal as a bringer of enlightenment and his growing realization that the savages he had come to convert and teach were themselves becoming both teachers and converters. He was afflicted with powerful desires and insatiable curiosity, with a capacity for self-condemnation and terrible remorse, and he tried desperately to reconcile his interest in the customs, the religion and the sexual mysteries of the Maoris with his own conventional Church of England background. It was no wonder that when he and his associates found themselves almost abandoned by the Church Missionary Society in far away London, left to fend for themselves and their families, the many temptations that assail exiles in an uncivilized country became too strong. They bartered muskets for food; the allurements of strong drink and brown women were an ever-present torment; and just as Kendall's spiritual life was thrown into confusion by his researches, so his domestic life was shattered by his constant wrestlings with the angels of darkness and of light. He was never quite sure that there was any easy way to distinguish between them.

It is to Sargeson's credit that he was able to identify himself with the complex personality of the ill-fated missionary who, in

Allen Curnow's words, "potently if enigmatically" prefigured "so
much that we have become";[8] and also that in the absence of
any theatrical tradition in New Zealand he could nonetheless
produce a moving play that, unorthodox as it is, can hold the
attention and involve an audience in a domestic situation which
carries implications beyond the personal relationships of the
protagonists. As the *New Zealand Listener* observed "to have
written a successful play in a country with a professional theatre
only intermittently alive is a considerable achievement." [9]

The theme of Thomas Kendall was not one that readily lent
itself to dramatic treatment, because those who have been impressed by what has been revealed of his private dilemmas have
not been primarily interested in what Kendall did nor in any of
the historical episodes in which he was involved. Although it is
possible that he may offer a subject for character in action, it is
rather as character in being that he becomes an extraordinary
figure. Therefore it is not surprising that Sargeson did not centre
his drama on any clear confrontation with the Church Missionary
Society or with Samuel Marsden, the senior chaplain in New
South Wales. He did not attempt to deal directly even with the
series of spiritual crises in the life of the disgraced missionary,
as the latter became more and more disturbed by his growing
awareness that the people he had come to convert and educate
were themselves possessed of a tradition and customs which,
alien as they were, enabled them to accept their environment
in a way that it was impossible for the few settlers to accept.
Sargeson devoted his attention not to the resolving of Kendall's
dilemmas, because these were incapable of being resolved, and
indeed were not resolved in his lifetime. He presented instead
a brief series of what could be called undramatic and domestic
episodes, and relied for interest and tension on the turns and
twists of the mind of his leading character in relation to his
wife, and his consciousness of the conflicting sets of values which
he was unable to reconcile. These were values that concerned
religion, manners, sex, and even topography and seasonal differences. In Sargeson's hands the undramatic becomes dramatic, the
episodic becomes a deeply moving survey of the past, the present,
and the future of Kendall's life in the Bay of Islands, and the
local and domestic is transformed into a vivid portrayal of

the predicament of uprooted humanity, aspiring greatly, failing dismally, in an antipodean purgatory. It is difficult not to be impressed by the following revelation of the soul of a man:

Kendall (*taking a drink, and then continuing as though not aware of any interruption*): When I am inquiring into the native religion, I do not willingly cease to be a Christian . . . neither do I discover myself to have become a heathen convert. . . . (*He raises first one arm, then the other, until he appears in the form of a cross*) But I find myself suspended, if you understand my meaning. I become like God himself, whom I judge to be ever impartial, and patient with all his children, when they try to understand him. . . . (*Richard and Johnson chink their money.*)[10]

The play opens at a point in time, some five years after the arrival of the Kendalls. The characters are few in number; and a Maori boy and girl together with a young Maori woman have very small parts. Besides Thomas and Jane Kendall there is the historical Richard Stockwell, ex-convict from Botany Bay and personal servant; but in addition Sargeson has created the un-historical but convincing Edwin Johnson, a runaway sailor, and the urbane and philosophical French captain of a visiting ship. The scene remains the same in each of the three acts—a sparsely furnished living room of the Kendalls with a few pictures on the walls including "the temptation of Adam by a coy and in-gratiating Eve." [11] Throughout the play action is almost non-existent and is limited to exits and entrances. This could well be regarded as a serious flaw in a drama that was concerned with spectacular theatre; but attention is riveted on Kendall's fluctu-ations of temper and emotion, on indications of attitude and activity revealed in the efficient dialogue on the relations be-tween Thomas and Jane Kendall and Richard Stockwell and on the desires of the last two to escape from the intolerable situa-tion in the Bay of Islands.

A Time for Sowing is, to use a much overworked term, 'a psychological drama,' one in which the adventures of the mind and the changes of emotion override external action, and the tension arises because, apart from the obvious liaison between Jane Kendall and Richard Stockwell, Kendall himself is always in the grips of despair or exalted by fervent faith. He is on the

verge of suicide, entangled between his deep love for his wife
and his love of the natives and their ways. He is the rigid
magistrate, the humane Christian missionary, the determined
anthropologist, teacher, grammarian, and drunkard, and a man
with a deep grievance because he is isolated from his Church
and because he is the cause of scandals that have been transmitted to his superiors overseas. He is arrogant and remorseful,
deeply humble and aware of his backslidings, tender, despair-
ing, and dictatorial by turns.

Sargeson has attempted a difficult task. He has converted into
a three-act play what might well have been the subject of a
long novel; yet by combining the dramatic interplay of language
with the small actions permitted by his form he has been able
to present a character in relation to other characters, and to
communicate the tensions and climaxes of a human being living
in his own private hell. This is subtly and movingly revealed
in the second act, immediately after Jane leaves the room with
Stockwell, ostensibly to meet her small children on the beach:

*(. . . their voices recede. For a moment Kendall remains listening at
the closed door, then he turns to the wine, but again replaces the
cork after pulling it. He looks again at the closed door, and as he
comes to the table begins to speak.)*

Kendall: Thy cheeks are comely. Oh let me lie betwixt thy breasts.
How much better is thy love than wine.

Repent. Repent. For the wages of sin is death. But you are fair my
beloved. Honey and milk are under thy tongue.

He that saith he hath no sin deceives himself. And there is no truth
in him. *(He goes to the sideboard and drinks wine from the bottle.)*

Thou hast ravished my heart. Thy two breasts are like two young roes
that are twins. Oh my beloved, my desire is toward thee.

Blessed are the pure in heart.

Repent. Repent of your sins before it is too late, and you are called
to judgment.

Repent. Repent. Repent.

*(At the table he picks up the Bible and throws it on the floor with
a loud bang. There is a long pause while he goes down on his knees.
He slowly picks up the Bible, and is standing with it when he starts
at the distant sound of a sea-shanty. He puts the Bible on the table
and goes for the musket.)* [12]

As a dramatic work of major importance *A Time for Sowing* suffers from serious limitations, not necessarily the result of the author's lack of skill nor of his failure to understand the requirements of good theatre. He makes heavy demands on producer, actors, and audience. An imperceptive producer working with a second-rate cast could reduce the stature of Thomas Kendall to that of a weak and vacillating character, whose changes in mood become trivial rather than tragic and incomprehensible rather than revealing. The other characters, including his wife, are able to perceive only the superficial sides of his nature—his unfaithfulness, his drunkenness, his involvement in pagan mysteries which seem to them despicable and obscene. An unimaginative production would be likely to turn him into a simple but pathetic playboy, inconstant, unpredictable, and irresponsible. Only superb acting would be able to convince even a sympathetic audience that the dialogues of which the play mainly consists have such close relevance to his inner struggles that the introduction of the runaway seaman and the captain of the French ship is able to contribute greatly to any conception of Kendall's attitude to sex and to philosophical and anthropological discoveries. These dialogues must never be allowed to turn into a sordid domestic argument, but should be transformed into what Sargeson himself has called a duel. It is a duel between the warring elements in Kendall's own breast, but one that can be disclosed only by means of the oppositions and parallels in the action and conversation. He is wrestling with the angel. He is struggling with his complex conscience and his desire to be true to deeply held convictions which ultimately are incompatible.

At a rehearsal-performance by members of a small amateur theatrical group in Auckland, a reviewer referred to "a damaging simplification" [13] and complained that Kendall did little more than talk and drink; but, in spite of what evidently was a poor production he was able to see that Sargeson had given "an example and a starting point for a drama out of our own New Zealand history." [14] Later, at the first full production—made possible by the Auckland Gallery Associates and the close collaboration between the producer, Christopher Cathcart, the designer of the set, Colin McCahon, and the author—another viewer, mildly critical of the theme of "Antipodean dilemma," was able to gain the impression that Sargeson's characters never became "mere symbols and (the play) can be considered to be a good example of the juxtaposition of characters who retain their reality as people while conveying the author's theme and satisfying the demands of form." [15] Certainly the reception to this series of performances by press and public must have been gratifying to the dramatist as well as indicative of the play's success both as entertainment and as a penetrating study of a dilemma that has wider relevance than to the life of Thomas Kendall.

III   The Cradle and the Egg

Although when Sargeson wrote about Capek's *Insect Play* he had maintained that anything fantastical was contrary to his habits of thought, the whole conception of *The Cradle and the Egg*, with its combination of determined realism, outrageous fantasy, and deliberate farce, makes it necessary to reject any suggestion that he was dogmatically opposed to the mingling of different modes of dramatic representation. The method he adopted may be condoned and even applauded in a drama that attempts to transcend the limits of time and place, progress from the parochial to the universal and develop into a cosmic comedy. It is a method, however, which must rely on Coleridge's willing suspension of disbelief before it can provide anything in the nature of significant entertainment. Sargeson has never repeated or imitated himself; and those readers who had vaguely expected that his second play would be another experiment in historical or psychological drama must have been disconcerted when it was presented by The New Independent Theatre for a series of six nights in June, 1962, under the direction, once again, of Christopher Cathcart.

With scant attention to any formal rules of dramatic construction, Sargeson devised each of his three acts in such a way that his audience was forced to adjust itself to the author's requirements and not to any of its own conceiving. Meaning and amusement could be obtained from the widely divergent scenes only by a recognition that the theme was indeed concerned with the cradle and the egg, that through man's age-long pilgrimage from

order to chaos and back again, destruction and creation have
become the only eternal verities, and that man's constant efforts
and persistent renewal provide the grand comedy of existence.

The first act of *The Cradle and the Egg* rather deceptively establishes an atmosphere of commendable realism by revealing
a conventional and old-fashioned living room in a coach builder's
house. The time is the early 1880's and the place a typical New
Zealand township. While a small boy asks questions of his
elders about the possibilities of flying in a balloon, the main
argument seems to concern the location of a proposed railway,
and the progress of the town from an age of coaches to the
modern age of steam. It ends with a conflagration, as sparks from
the pipe of the self-styled "progressive" store-keeper ignite the
wooden building owned by the conservative coach builder, and
in the ensuing turmoil the latter rescues not only his baby in its
cradle but also a monstrous Easter egg which he has cherished
for many years.

The second act abruptly and necessarily abandons the earlier
set of characters for the passengers on an aeroplane in mid-
flight, some seventy years later. Among these are a strange old
man, who reveals that he lives on an island and is soon discovered to be the original baby of the first act, a youthful poet
who lives in the present and the past, an engineer who looks to
the future and has found "a damn good religion. . . . a religion
a scientist can believe in," [16] together with a bright and sophisticated young woman. Throughout the act the engineer plays
with an egg-shaped object of "a tarnished silver colour and
rather bigger than a duck egg," [17] a Mills bomb. As the curtain
falls (or there is a blackout) passengers, crew, and another
baby in its cradle are blown to pieces by the explosion caused
when the engineer dashes his toy to the floor.

In the final act, the music of the spheres is faintly heard from
a rock somewhere in space, at no particular time in the far-off
future. A young poet, who has characteristics resembling those
of an evangelistic schoolteacher in the first act, the engineer
whose conversation had been concerned with science, sex, and
religion, and the young woman who was the centre of attention
in the second act are the sole inhabitants of the rock. In a cradle-
like hollow, however, lies a huge egg, the size of a football,

which is being carefully guarded by the woman. This final act concludes with the world, distantly seen between the sun and the moon, beginning to cool after it has burned for some millions of years; and as the curtain falls the woman and the two men walk off and *"the egg appears to glow with a radiance of its own."* [18]

Through the whole course of the play there is no attempt to stress the fantastic or the supernatural. For the purposes of cosmic drama little difficulty is experienced in accepting that the baby in the cradle in the 1880's has become the old man on the aeroplane who has spent his life in isolation on an island or that in the last act it is his voice that is heard as though coming through a loudspeaker to the three dead-alive people on the rock. The conversation and the arguments are conducted in a straightforward, idiomatic, witty and very human manner, whether the speakers are earthbound or somewhere in space. The dialogue arises naturally from the situation and the personalities of the characters, but revolves round subjects that have troubled human beings since life began—religion, sex and local politics, progress and retrogression, the claims of mind and of heart, the search for the new and the preservation of the old. Time may leap forward and finally collapse, but the characters, whoever they may be or under whatever conditions they may find themselves, are enclosed by sameness in the midst of infinite variety, for always discussion and action repeat themselves at different levels. The businessman, the scientist, the poet, the lover, the idealist and the seeker after religious truth, together with those who insist on turning life into a mathematical equation and those who convert it into feeling and sentiment, the bored, the disillusioned, the superficial, and the trivial materialist are to be found in all ages and in all environments; but always there is the cradle and the egg. Creation is a continual process that operates despite the limitations imposed by small-town life, by scientific discovery and destructive thought or by death on a rock lost in the eternity of space.

Nevertheless *The Cradle and the Egg* is more than a series of spectacular tableaux depicting the cycle of renewal and decay. Its theme, but not its comic significance, may be indicated by the following passage of dialogue which takes place on the barren rock.

Ernest (*to Stephanie*). There's just one thing. (*She makes an impatient gesture*) No, please don't think it's anything personal. You mentioned the Old Man, and it must be thousands of years since any of us have seen him. Where is he? What's he up to?

Stephanie. Search me. But I imagine he's about his business. No doubt he's somewhere around the cosmos.

Ernest. But what *is* his business, Stephanie? I've often wondered. Does he actually run the cosmos?

Stephanie. Do you suppose he is somebody out of a comic strip? . . . Nobody runs the cosmos. Nobody has to. The cosmos is a creation. Every creation has a life of its own. As it is with that egg, or with Antony's poems for that matter, so it is with the cosmos. . . . But death is the natural corollary to the gift of creation. Having passed on life to the creation, the creator dies. . . . Shall I tell you a great mystery? . . . So long as creation is perpetually renewed, there is always the perpetual possibility that creation will achieve its sublime purpose . . . that is to say, will re-create its original creator. . . . Do you wonder that I guard the egg? . . .[19]

This is a theme that links the creative arts to the secret of the egg; and from one point of view the whole play can be regarded as a dramatic representation of what Coleridge called the primary imagination—"a repetition in the finite mind of the eternal act of creation in the infinite I AM."

Such an exposition neglects the essential nature of what is after all a comedy, even if it is a cosmic comedy. Reviewing the first performance of the play for *Landfall*, Bruce Beaver claimed that it "proved both an innovation in style and an imaginative advance in form to the highly appreciative audience," [20] which suggests that it became "good theatre" in spite of its unorthodox structure and the ontological problems its theme may appear to involve. Some of the reasons for its success are that, although the characters are without depth or subtlety, they are completely individualized, and Sargeson is able to devise dialogue that is both dramatic and comic. Irony and social satire are all-pervasive. Symbols like the Easter egg, the flowering plum tree and the all-consuming fire are used lightly, but with telling effect. The continual references and cross-references to ideas associated with past and future, with nature, creation, and resurrection provide sufficient clues to restrain an audience from mistaking a serious play for a bizarre exhibition of virtuosity; and the original characters of the first act are not forgotten, for their fates are revealed by the baby who had slept through their disputes and anticipations of coming events.

Sargeson's sense of comedy has always been neglected because of the attention paid to his role of innovator and his treatment, particularly in the short story, of important aspects of New Zealand life and attitude. *The Cradle and the Egg* is what Polonius might have described as "tragical-comical-historical-pastoral," but the emphasis is on high comedy, for Sargeson is a skilful contriver of comic episodes, as short stories like *A Man and his Wife, The Hole that Jack Dug,* and *A Man of Good Will,* as well as many passages in *I Saw in My Dream,* amply illustrate. In *Up onto the Roof and Down Again* he had once listed some of the questions he was continually being asked by well-intentioned people troubled by his attitudes to conventional behaviour and customary modes of living. Among these were: "Why do I answer back with quotations out of the Bible when I have left off going to church and haven't a spark of religion in me? Why am I always joking? Why do I persist in being cheerful over serious matters?" Sargeson has always been attracted to man's fumbling attempts to encompass the meaning of life in myth, creed, and dogma, but as *The Cradle and the Egg* clearly reveals, his own conception is more closely related to a preoccupation with the process and the implications of creative endeavour. This in no way prevents him from finding comedy in the tragic experience of living and, to the bewilderment of those people who are apt to mistake a lively sense of the ludicrous for mere flippancy or cynicism, he persists not only in "being cheerful over serious matters," but in employing humour, whether ribald, grotesque, or subtle, in order to convey the peculiar flavour of a situation, a personality or a variety of utterance.

The witticisms of *The Cradle and the Egg,* even the "bromides" consciously used by some of his characters, have no tendency to pall or to irritate, because they contribute to rather than detract from the seriousness of the dramatized theme. Bruce Beaver was right when he wrote of the third act "even in the most desolate of settings the characters still appear to be at home—indeed like several prodigious infants playing Mums and Dads on a Brobdingnagian scale." [21] With a writer who, like Falstaff, was able to see man as "a forked radish, with a head fantastically carved," and to derive pleasure as well as significance from the unpredictable activities of human beings, the possibility has always existed that he would try his skill at writing a genuinely comic and full-length novel. After his excursions in the dramatic form contained in *Wrestling with the Angel*, Sargeson published in 1965 his *Memoirs of a Peon*.

CHAPTER 8

Casanova in Auckland

"Who could be anything more in such a country?"

I *The Picaresque Tradition*

IN HIS SHORT stories, and particularly in *That Summer,* there are indications that Sargeson has always been attracted to aspects of the novel that lie within the picaresque tradition. Joyce Cary and Kingsley Amis among other writers found considerable advantages in revitalizing an ancient form that, although far removed from the early Spanish examples, had a distant relation to the eighteenth-century *Moll Flanders* and *Roderick Random.* With whatever distinctive qualities they might possess, Gulley Jimson and Jim Dixon behaved at times like irresponsible rogues, whose surprising and ridiculous adventures provided a caustic if hilarious commentary on some important facets of modern civilization.

The narrator of Sargeson's *That Summer* had recounted in a series of loosely connected scenes and conversations his slightly less spectacular experiences in a New Zealand city, but the brevity of the novel had helped to disguise its marked resemblances to the picaresque. It was, therefore, not altogether unexpected that the creator of the tough but sentimental Bill should sooner or later experiment at greater length with a story which looked back both to the memoirs of various fictional rogues and to those of the celebrated Casanova. By adopting the mask of one Michael Newhouse, born in Hamilton and later of Auckland, the King Country and Rotorua; by the extraordinary consistency of his first-person narrative; and by a further development of his characteristic techniques, he captured the flavour of a mode of writing largely discarded, in order to cast reflections on contemporary New Zealand attitudes. The result proved to be an extended comic novel, episodic in structure and centred

148

on the amatory adventures of a social nonconformist who was convinced that his talents, both sexual and literary, deserved recognition by the antipodean society he held in great contempt.

Many of Sargeson's characters, like those in the early picaresque novels, had been wanderers, without roots in the established society around them. If they had not been reckless rogues or disreputable self-seekers, they had shown an incapacity to adjust themselves for long to the conditions imposed on them by routine occupations and suburban family life. As by implication the *picaro* had been a virtual outcast from feudal society, so the casual workers of Sargeson's stories, without any coherent philosophy or orderly process of thinking, had rejected the attitudes of a falsely puritanical and money-conscious middle class that worshipped status symbols and all evidences of material progress and success. Although his narrative technique had almost wholly excluded opportunities for authorial intrusion, it was always apparent both from his selection and treatment that his books were filled with criticism and condemnation of ways of living that emphasized the mechanical at the expense of the creative. He was ever ready to ridicule what others would regard as the sanctities of bourgeois behaviour and to expose the shallowness of all assumptions which ignored human values and sensitivity. Even his *Memoirs of a Peon* is introduced by a satirical comment supposedly derived from "Talks with a Bodgie": "I asked what he meant by describing the man at the wheel of the Jaguar as a peon. 'Of course he's a peon,' he replied. 'He works just as hard, doesn't he? And I'll bet he never has a quarter the fun.'" [1]

Sargeson's standards of reference may be heard to determine, but only because he is neither a clumsy moralist nor a refined cynic, and in his imaginative writing has refused to commit himself to philosophic or political affirmations. He has been content to remain an artistic outsider, exercising his inalienable right to explore the effects on the human personality of the society for which he has little reverence. Nevertheless, he has always been drawn towards a sympathetic portrayal of the despised and rejected; and if his work contains within it anarchical tendencies and a sardonic refusal to admit that social progress can be achieved by animated cogs in a monstrous machine, it has been invariably humane and sensitive to the emotional aspirations of his waifs and strays. As *I Saw in My Dream* and *The Cradle and the Egg* clearly reveal, the scale of values that emerges from his writing is one that places its main emphasis on the creative instinct. Any suppression or distortion of this instinct in private or in social life provokes his anger and provides much of the material for his dramatic representations and concealed commentary.

In the preface to *Roderick Random* Smollett had complained of his picaresque model that

> the disgraces of Gil Blas are, for the most part, such as rather excite mirth than compassion: he himself laughs at them; and his transitions from distress to happiness, or at least ease, are so sudden, that neither the reader has time to pity him, nor himself to be acquainted with affliction. This conduct, in my opinion, not only deviates from probability, but prevents that generous indignation which ought to animate the reader against the sordid and vicious disposition of the world.

Despite the limitations of the first-person narrative and the unprepossessing qualities of his self-centred and pugnacious hero, Smollett manages to deliver many of his moral blows at society with a literary sledge hammer, and demonstrates his jaundiced preoccupation with "the selfishness, envy, malice and base indifference of the world." Sargeson is more ambiguous in his attitude and far more subtle and sophisticated in his techniques, with the result that he is often in danger of confusing and irritating his readers by an attention to detail that may seem irrelevant, and a narrative method that reduces the impact of event and the comedy of outrageous situation.

II   *The Cultural Cringe*

To a considerable extent *Memoirs of a Peon* disappoints any expectations aroused by its resemblance to the picaresque mode. Although it has more than its share of erotic interludes and scandalous intrigues, it is likely to be appreciated more fully by those who are able to derive enjoyment from the ironic delineation of character and the deliberately chosen and consistently maintained style of the narrator. The aim has been not merely to devise a series of involved and ridiculous situations, nor to produce a fast-moving tale of misadventures that will propel the reader forward from incident to incident, but to cast an oblique light on the New Zealand scene by focussing attention on an egocentric and bizarre human being who, because of his atypical qualities and literary interests, feels himself superior to the people who have easily adjusted themselves to their provincial and tasteless environment.

The choice of Michael Newhouse as the main protagonist and narrator of *Memoirs of a Peon* might seem strange to anyone who had carefully followed Sargeson's career from the time when he wrote the brief stories on which his early reputation was founded. It might seem stranger still to those who had heard his radio talk on "Writing a Novel," in which he disclosed his confirmed prejudice in favour of what he called "the material of New Zealand life" and his hope that he would be able to discover and create "a suitable hero." The escapades of a modern small-town Casanova no doubt would present excellent opportunities to a novelist intent on catching the attention of a reading public unable to resist stories of sexual adventures and comic entanglements but not, it might be thought, to one who was determined to restrict himself to the activities and attitudes of "representative New Zealanders" and regarded himself as a realist.

The language in which the book is written is quite obviously a departure from Sargeson's idiomatic and unpretentious style; and the succession of absurd and slightly salacious episodes can scarcely be described as typical of the behaviour of the majority of his countrymen and women. It is difficult to imagine any "kiwi" stereotype attending a Marriage Defense League meeting in the company of a woman whose virtue had excited his sensual appetite, and indulging in a reverie conveyed in these terms:

I recollected that a touch of duplicity, or at any rate self-deception, though of course rightly handled, had been characteristic of some of the most saintly figures in history; and I remember that we arrived at our destination while I was thinking of Saint Teresa, whose love affair with God, no matter how acceptable to the Church it was eventually adjudged to be, does not by any means appear to have been wholly purged of all the dross of carnality: though I hasten to add that I am at all times ready to take off my hat to this most

practical saint, and it is not at all my intention to suggest that she is
to be numbered among those antinomian heretics who may be grossly
misled by too much confidence in the certainty of their election.[2]

The Sargeson of the early stories cannot be recognized in the
sentence structure and deliberate pedantry of the following passage, which recalls some of the learned comments of Uncle
Hilary:

I remember they touched a great deal upon the question of trans-
lations from the classics: Byron's useful renderings from Catullus for
example; and his endearing but quite unsatisfactory shot at *Animula
vagula;* Milton's quite miraculous beginning when he essayed Horace's
fifth ode; and the innumerable attempts by various hands at the
palatinate anthology and the Sapphic fragments. (It dismayed me
infinitely to hear my uncle's Alas! when I owned to virtually no
Greek, and to imagine that I discovered in his glance a profound
sadness. "Perhaps it may not be too late to remedy that," he remarked.
"Perhaps you may prove to be an opsimath." But I construed his
words as a mere politeness.)[3]

The slightly mannered and formal style used by Michael Newhouse to record his amoral activities in what his English friend,
following Smollett, calls an age of roguery is likely to be fully
appreciated only by those who are willing and able to perceive
that *Memoirs of a Peon* depends for its effect on the personality
of the hero and the complex organization of what at first sight
seems to be a straightforward picaresque novel. It is necessary
to grasp all the implications that stem from the fact that the
well-to-do and aging "Peon" who is "stung with the snake of
memory"[4] is recalling the events of his youth, more than forty
years in the past. With wry humour and affecting a mode of
utterance that has become habitual, he not only attempts to describe the responses of the raw, inexperienced and vainglorious
youngster to the world into which he had been born but also, as
a crusty and disillusioned old man, an unrepentant parasite and
discontented social conformer, to comment on the changed environment from which the glamour has departed.

He remembers himself as a short, stocky youth with low brow,
heavy chin and the unprepossessing face of a pugilist, but en-

dowed with an overweening pride in his potentialities as scholar and irresistible lover. In his old age he has become corpulent and embittered, exhibiting many of the physical defects of advanced years, and neither his spectacles nor the knee-breeches he chooses to wear can disguise the deterioration of his outward appearance. The reader is intended to be concerned at one and the same time with these two characters, actor and narrator: the young man, bumptious, confident and scornful of the inferior aspirations of his fellow creatures, and the older, less resilient, more prejudiced and disillusioned, but critically aware of the immaturity and deficiencies of his earlier self. Despite his lack of any real achievement, he is still convinced, however, of the mental improverishment and mediocrity of his human surroundings. In his boyhood he had been greatly influenced by an elderly and studious lawyer who was content to earn his living by selling confectionery.

Ernie's years of study had proved his undoing: he had taken a look into the world of learning and decided that he was a citizen of that world by vocation. Not that he could be described as anything but a smatterer, he used to say; but who could be anything more in such a country, where one was lucky to lay hands on about ten out of every hundred books one wanted to read?[5]

It is this tone of "who could be anything more in such a country" that pervades the *Memoirs of a Peon,* but the double-edged satire of the book is emphasized when the reader observes that the comments of the older Newhouse, cleverly interwoven as they are with the imperfect but vivid recollections of his earlier responses to experience, do not always coincide with the younger man's impressions. It is true that the narrator is able to maintain a measure of critical detachment from the impudent and conceited behaviour of the actor in events forty years in the past; but, to complicate matters, it is also apparent that the latter is sometimes able to recognize that he has cut a poor figure in the conduct of his intrigues, and that his actions do not always confirm his assumptions of superiority and genius. It is part of Sargeson's aim that the mature, if eccentric, reflections of the elderly insurance inspector should be mingled with what seems to be the record of a young man's immediate experience. Both

reflections and record touch at many points the quality of New
Zealand life and provide a lively and complex commentary on
the shortcomings of an island culture and the habits of a people
preoccupied with the commonplace details of material advancement.

It is this combination, rendered more intricate by the reader's
apprehension that the attitudes of other characters in the novel
are often at variance with those of the younger and older Newhouse, that helps to extend the layers of comedy and enriches
an irony not altogether in keeping with the less sophisticated
picaresque tradition. When the young philanderer is on a paint-
ing expedition with the wealthy Gower-Johnson he finds it
deeply depressing to gaze either at the amateur painter or at
his picture, which had carefully washed out any reminder of
"harsh and unrelenting sunlight, of the desolate terror of those
frowning heights or that wilderness of scrub." [6] Newhouse continues his meditations by confessing "I miserably began . . . to
review my past life and inquire whether I might not be as hopelessly mistaken about the large matters I occupied myself with
as Mr. Gower-Johnson had that afternoon proved himself to
be." It is these large matters that are constantly contrasted with
the banal and trivial activities of less ambitious New Zealanders
who so obviously demonstrate their indifference to intellectual
and aesthetic pursuits.

At an early stage in his career Michael Newhouse had decided
that he was like Hans Andersen's young man, who was imperfectly changed from a swan and retained a wing instead of an
arm. Brought up by his grandmother and associating generally
with adults who had varying degrees of scholarly attainments,
he had begun to speak a literary language that caused astonishment to his rather infrequent playmates. At secondary school
in Hamilton he had become more than usually friendly with
an exceptional school mistress who, as the old man recalled, had
declared that

. . . human life had been robbed of its traditional meaning by the
decay of religion, so what we were faced with was strictly speaking
only one problem—what to occupy ourselves with as adults so that
we might meet our daily expenses, and at the same time make the

richest possible use of our lives in the prevailing circumstances: and part of that use of our lives would be a constant endeavour to understand our environment even though we could not hope to escape from it. There was nonetheless always the chance that we might prove ourselves gifted with the heroic virtues by engaging ourselves upon a strenuous attempt to change our environment.[7]

It is evident, even from this remembered utterance of a minor character, that the comedy of contrived adventures is not intended to engross the whole attention of the reader. As in his other writings Sargeson is still concerned with an exploration of human attitudes to surroundings that, although not confined to New Zealand, are peculiarly local and individual. His own opinions are disguised and transformed by the variety of personal views held by the people among whom Michael Newhouse moves on his disorderly journey from childhood to youth. There is no more reason to assume that the advice to reject the commonplace "in favour of a single-minded endeavour at improvement in matters of taste and understanding"[8] comes directly from the author than it is to credit him with the statement that "sedentary occupations which produce no tangible or financially profitable results are an idle and unhealthy waste of time."[9]

The amorous diversions and dubious practices of the small-town Casanova are described with gusto, but in a style that is full of literary allusion and what may be mistaken for verbal mannerism. With an ear sensitive to the habits of speech in eighteenth-century English novels, Sargeson creates a language that harmonizes with the bookish disposition of his hero. This is not a useless exhibition of a writer's virtuosity, but a deliberately devised part of his intention. Some readers, unaware of the skill with which he has adopted words, phrases, and sentence structure that belong to an earlier tradition, may be more irritated than delighted with the linguistic pastiche. Others, however, will perceive that the figure of Michael Newhouse becomes a comic representation of the "cultural cringe" to which reference has already been made. The language of his recollections is absurdly suited to one who is convinced that he is well qualified to move in distinguished circles, but has become "hopelessly bogged down in an environment much too raw to exhibit even the rudiments of civilization."[10]

III *Comedy of Manners*

Nevertheless, any significance *Memoirs of a Peon* may have
arises mainly from the light-hearted treatment of the mental
and moral climate of a land and its people. Newhouse is quick
to condemn the triviality and mediocrity of his surroundings,
but he gives little sign that what he regards as his unacknowledged genius is more than a pale reflection of his inordinate
vanity. Grown old, he is still caustic in his comments, although
at the same time better able to recognize his former immaturity,
but the perceptive reader becomes increasingly aware that Newhouse, old or young, is not altogether a reliable witness. He is
as much the subject of the comic spirit's laughter as those aspects
of New Zealand which provoke his own mockery. His accumu-
lation of knowledge brings to him neither happiness nor wisdom,
and by the end of the book he is no nearer his professed goal
of satisfying his intellectual curiosity by dabbling in those larger
and nebulous matters that had constituted his purpose in life.

The worldly success which he had affected to despise has
been thrust on him rather than achieved, and he has become
vaguely conscious that he has been both a pawn and a peon,
manipulated by social forces beyond his control and embittered
by a society that steadfastly refuses to pay tribute to his small
attainments. His memoirs are so constructed that the reader is
all the time being involved in a protracted and critical argument about life in a newly developed country. Because he is
led by the events and the relations between the characters to
see more and to understand more than the self-centred narrator,
he is able to obtain an unusual view of the social influences
that contribute to the making of a New Zealander. For the first
time, Sargeson has attempted to create a character whose condemnation of provincialism happily burlesques the supercilious
strictures of the intellectual outsider. Although born and bred
in the Waikato, Michael Newhouse belongs by choice to an
alien tradition and finds it impossible to identify himself with
the inhabitants of a country which, in his opinion, pays scant
attention to the art of living. Nevertheless, his commentary on
New Zealand is also a commentary on himself. He is both hero

and anti-hero of a comedy of manners which treats critic and the objects of his criticism with equal irony and amusement.

In his affairs with women the aspiring Casanova sooner or later discovers that, although his vigorous carnal appetite may be gratified, he has been relegated to the position of a slightly ridiculous and pathetic victim by a female astuteness with which he is generally unable to compete. His performances as a gastropod, when in order to approach the fascinating dress-designer in an adjoining apartment he is forced to make what he calls a "preliminary gesture of abasement" [11] by crawling between two wooden urns on the balcony, is characteristic of situations in which he continually finds himself. In his discussions with acquaintances he fares no better. His familiarity with an assortment of ancient writings and philosophical or theological disputes enhances his opinion of himself without increasing his ability to pass examinations or to improve his arguments with those less informed on abstract questions; but the memories of the more mature Newhouse are made more piquant by the realization that he himself had been as callow as the specimens of humanity to whom he had applied the same contemptuous epithet.

His experiences of life in a New Zealand city are greatly diversified because he is compelled by the frequent difficulties of his financial and amatory affairs to make repeated changes in his mode of living. In the course of a few years he transfers himself and his precious books (many of which have been stolen) from a Friendly Society Hostel in Auckland to a suburban area in Ponsonby, and from there to a furnished room in Lower Symonds Street. Before he revisits his Hamilton relatives and for a brief period takes inefficient charge of a one-teacher school in the King Country, he is reduced to the level of occupying a cellar in the slum district of Freeman's Bay. These changes in location serve the useful purpose of increasing his awareness of how other people live and of expanding his knowledge of some of the less reputable activities of an odd collection of human beings. Although sometimes they may interfere with his literary studies, they are usually accompanied by new directions in his subsidiary interests.

He has what he calls his religious year when with little profit he attends lectures at the university and lodges at the hostel supported by the wealthy sectarian, Gower-Johnson. This early portion of the *Memoirs* is concerned not only with his attempt to conduct a double intrigue with Mrs. Gower-Johnson and her daughter, but also with a number of episodes which reveal the false puritanism that, according to Sargeson, is a marked feature of contemporary society in New Zealand. The young Newhouse is influenced by the Venerable Bede in coming to the conclusion that Christianity is "an unbalanced religion, because it is heavily committed to approving only what might be described as the daylight behaviour of human beings: that is to say, it is a religion which exhibits an Apollonian character powerful enough to drive into obscurity, if it does not totally exclude, all Dionysiac elements." [12] With perverse and pedantic ingenuity he continues throughout the book to expose and comment on the open or disguised sensuality made manifest in his many encounters with male, and particularly female, acquaintances. *Memoirs of a Peon* thus becomes a double-pronged satire on antipodean morality. Because of the idiosyncratic attributes of the narrator it is slanted both towards a demonstration of the concealed but welcome depravity of an island people and towards a review of their tasteless and uncivilized surroundings.

The sporting year of Michael Newhouse, necessary to even a cursory examination of dominant attitudes of the average New Zealander, is spent in association with the Ponsonby Meiklejohns: "it was surely calamitous that by becoming in appearance and perhaps even in identity a Meiklejohn I had put myself back almost exactly where I had started from. My most troubling moments would derive from the thought that if I was by nature an undoubted Meiklejohn even though I had never previously known it, then people such as Ernie and Margaret had been the mistakes of my life." [13] It is here, among young and retired athletes, that he learns the use of chest expanders and gripbells, runs several miles each morning, and engages in regular gymnasium and football training under the guidance of two of the many grotesque characters humorously described by the malicious aspirant for athletic honours. His unaccustomed exertions make considerable inroads on the time he can devote to serious reading, but his experiences of the conversation, behaviour, and ambitions of these new suburban acquaintances provide many occasions for disparaging remarks about the quality of New Zealand life, combined with regret that his grandparents had chosen to leave a country much closer to the haunts of gentility and the liberal arts.

Because of the way in which *Memoirs of a Peon* has been conceived, the characters that throng its pages are more often exaggerated oddities than the realistic portraits with which Sargeson was chiefly concerned in his earlier writings. In keeping with the picaresque tradition that includes Smollett and to some extent even Dickens, they are described in terms of their physical peculiarities and mental quirks. There is the lecherous grave digger in Hamilton who discourses on life and death and for five shillings and a stolen smoked fish acts as procurer for the adolescent Newhouse and his companion. Uncle Hilary, with his short leg and withered arm, smells of brandy and lives secluded in an upstairs room, which is littered with books and artificial aids to restore his mutilated face. The follower of Bakunin emerges from his cave-like dwelling behind a printing establishment only to visit hotel and library, and Mr. Crepitt in leopard skin and sandshoes resembles one of Michelangelo's supermen as he delivers his homilies on health living. The wiry little midlander who had manufactured doll's eyes for many years, the antipodean Semiramis, Lenora Greenbatch, with pneumatic bust and camphor-scented rabbit fur, the diminutive Mr. Ritchie, erudite celebrant of married love, whose complexion was like that of a wax model—all these and many others make their brief appearances in a novel that demonstrates its author's ability to create character with a few deft strokes in order to suit his theme and satiric purpose.

The rooms and houses, the very districts in which they live become, as in Dickens, extensions of their personalities, and it would be possible for some readers to return with anticipated pleasure to scores of passages only to recapture the atmosphere of vivid detail in which the scenes are presented. Among other examples it is not easy for a New Zealander to forget the description given by Newhouse of one of those antiquated institutions which used to be so common in the cities:

. . . the dingy, old, high-gabled school building with its bare floors which were thumped by boots and scuffed by bare feet, the echoing corridors made dim by the capacity of wall-paint to digest the dust and dirt of generations, the pot-holed asphalt playground where the stale crusts hardened in the sun if they were kicked about too long before the scruffy sparrows got them.[14]

His account of the post-funeral party he attended, with the women segregated in the parlour and the men drinking beer in the gas-lit kitchen, suggests a remarkable similarity to other parties at which he was present in later years:

The tall rowing brother was a racehorse compared to the monolithic footballer; and although the other two had been sawn off short, the dirt track rider was as lithesome as a monkey when put alongside the squat and muscle-bound pugilist. There were unifying appearances, nevertheless, which in addition made them much of a muchness with all the young men in the room. All had the same style of haircut, for example, and three piece suits were the rule—though jackets had been discarded and waistcoats unbuttoned, and I was interested to note the apparently fashionable use of steel-spring armbands to shorten shirt-sleeves.[15]

Literary parallels and classical references are always in the mind of the young hero, and frequently his keen perceptions are mingled with memories of passages from the books he is always reading, so that his record of incidents gives both the impression of immediacy and the flavour of a by-gone age. It is as though New Zealand is being looked at for the first time by one who is the degenerate heir to a tradition that has been deliberately abandoned in the country of his birth.

The climax of the studious Casanova's success arrives after his sudden departure from Ponsonby. The money he succeeds in appropriating from the dishonest son of Lenora Greenbatch is enough to keep him in comparative comfort when supplemented by his teacher's salary. For different periods of time he enjoys the physical attentions of two mistresses and then when he enters the training college he spends a theatrical and political year rehearsing as Caliban for a performance of *The Tempest* and producing pamphlets with a group of dedicated Marxists.

The latter occupation leads to his friendship with the family of the former manufacturer of doll's eyes and, after his money has disappeared and his lovers vanished, to his tenancy of a basement room in Freeman's Bay. These events offer further opportunities for satiric commentary and comic description as well as social analysis, but the book tends to become more and more episodic and disjointed. Newhouse's eccentricities of dress, his failure as an actor, his brief flirtation with revolutionary thought and activity, his rediscovery of Uncle Hilary and his slight contact with drug addicts and homosexuals are too rapidly passed over to add greatly to the significance of his memoirs.

There is, indeed, no reason why a picaresque novel with a plot that is merely a succession of characters and entertaining incidents should ever end, except through the exhaustion of writer or reader. Nevertheless, it is a defect of *Memoirs of a Peon* that it begins to disintegrate as the attempt is made to draw together the tenuous threads of the story. Sargeson seems anxious to conclude his unusual experiment and conducts his hero through a number of disconnected but amusing experiences before returning him to Auckland and an uncomfortable refuge in the ceiling of a tramway shelter shed. He visits his family in Hamilton and discovers that his farming brother is almost the only contented person he has met during his vagabondage. He teaches in a school beyond Te Kuiti and is dismissed by the inspector. He works on a farm and is seduced by the farmer's wife. He arrives in the Hutt valley and helps a tomato grower "dedicated to the search for a solution to the problems of social organization, but with the additional obsession that he might possibly, if he tried hard enough, discover the truth about human destiny."[16] Finally he descends from the roof of the tram shelter in Auckland into the arms of Betty Gower-Johnson.

As in *Roderick Random* coincidences abound and characters disappear, leaving no trace. A very few of them are woven into the plot, which keeps losing itself in authentic detail and ridiculous interlude. In such a novel it is scarcely surprising that the secretive Yorkshireman who had advised Newhouse in his Friendly Society Hostel days should become the husband of Gower-Johnson's widow, nor that the tangle of weeds in the backgarden where Michael spent some of his boyhood years should prove to be the Indian hemp used for the marijuana orgies which were held in a room below Uncle Hilary's library. The value of *Memoirs of a Peon* depends not on its successful revival of the picaresque mode, but on its achievement as a complex satire and a comic novel that might well write "finis" to all those essays and books that continue to belabour the well-worn theme of the provincial dullness and aesthetic immaturity of New Zealand.

CHAPTER 9

A Note on The Hangover *(1967)*

Aladdin in the Basements

When we are frozen up within, and quite
The phantom of ourselves.

MATTHEW ARNOLD

"IN these pages I try to justify . . ." The sentence remains unfinished, hovering on the brink of "a tremendous sub-stantive" which in another place is spelt out as "my life"; and although the incompleted fragment is repeated more than once in the journal of a central character in *The Hangover*, there is a sense in which it can be attributed to the author, and not only to the superannuated beatnik with bucket and mop. This deceptively simple novel resolves itself into a reaffirmation of attitudes implicit in Sargeson's imaginative rendering of the human situation from the early short stories to *Memoirs of a Peon*.

At the plot level *The Hangover* is concerned with an explora-tion of disturbed adolescence, with the disintegration of the human personality when a debased puritanism collides with a forgotten world of sensation and feeling, with the failure to adjust the order of childhood innocence to the disorder of adult experience; but it is much more than this. It is a vivid dramatiza-tion of the dichotomies of life, a commentary on the affluent society of the technocrats, an anatomy of the outsider, the beat-nik generation and the "elongated hangover from Socrates and the Academy." It is an examination of the reasons why man, wrapped in his protective coverings, is little more than a nervous onion, and in modern times Arnold's "frozen up within" applies to both young and old.

If such an account of the successor to *Memoirs of a Peon* would seem to stress its philosophical and social implications at

the expense of its narrative qualities, this is because Sargeson
has made little attempt to provide a detailed and realistic background to a story that, although it moves swiftly to a horrifying
conclusion, weaves its way through a complex pattern of objective correlatives, literary analogues and fragments of myth and
ritual. The incidents, the places, the human beings are not ones
that offer much opportunity to evoke either the New Zealand
scene or character. As so often with Sargeson, despite his ability to communicate the realities of sight and sound, he tends to
translate the actual into the mythical, and one is reminded again
of the observation: "a reflection of the world he wrote from, a
comment on it, but not that world." He is neither an uncom-
promising social realist nor a writer of allegorical fictions, and
his use of symbols has always been sparing and possibly un-
planned. His awareness of correspondences, however, is such
that his apprehension and criticism of life are continually en-
riched by meanings that arise from the contemplation of parallels and analogies.

If the story of Aladdin and his lamp is important to the
structure of *The Hangover* it is used suggestively rather than
mechanically. It is true that Alan whose discoveries and confusions are the theme of the novel has a name that happily reminds
his hard-working mother of the well-remembered Arabian tale,
that he thinks of engineering studies in terms of an earlier magic
that can cause the disappearance of social barriers insurmount-
able to his parents, and that later he believes that in a very
different fashion he has discovered the secret meaning of the
enchanted lamp, a meaning that has nothing to do with palaces,
jewels and a Sultan's daughter. Nevertheless, although his discovery is the result of experiences in the cave-like cellars frequented by beatniks and their associates, the Aladdin story is
almost forgotten as cellars and basements proliferate and symbolic counters cluster and multiply.

The journal of the self-justifying Dick Lennie who tries to
look at life without illusions is matched by the incredible
"Threefold Path" which Dottie, at one time resembling a great
kitchen goddess, at another a stone woman in an Indian temple,
is writing in her disorderly house. Below in a concrete basement
Jasper, one of her fancy-boys, reads *The New Atlantis* or *The*

Decline of the West and in his grubby underpants makes something human from perforated metal strips. In another basement,
well-appointed this time, Geoffrey arranges and polishes his
buttons which have the virtue of both revealing as well as con-
cealing. Arcady, the Earthly Paradise and the age of innocence
are evoked behind the rubbish in the backyard of a derelict
house in Lancaster Lane by Solly, the angelic beatnik who could
not take the university and who gives a new twist to the story
of the barren figtree. It is Solly also who expounds Marvell's
"Had we but world enough, and time" to his two friends in a
sleeping bag.

Nothing is what it seems in this phantasmagoria of bizarre
figures and erratic behaviour. Innocence and experience are in-
terchangeable; no purity remains unsullied; human beings live
out abstractions rather than engage in living; they chase shadows
in a world of substitutes; and their actions fall into ritualistic
patterns that convert truth into deception and deception into
truth. Alan, at first obsessed with the evil of the elderly beatnik,
dimly conscious that the order of his innocent childhood has
been based on a lie, and confused by the illusion of appearances, dons his plastic coats and proceeds to destroy those in
whom the dichotomies of life are most disturbing to his dis-
ordered mind. He tells himself that there is nothing personal in
his action, and here he is right. As Dick Lennie surmises, he
may be a human being, but he is not a person; and a personal
relation in any true sense of the term has been robbed of any
meaning it might have possessed.

A conflict of attitudes is usually the starting-point for Sargeson's explorations of a society in which "negation has all the
force of what is positive." He has little sympathy with those
whose creed has become one of life-denying prohibitions and
whose virtues are the achievements of a narrow respectability.
In so far as he identifies himself with any of his characters it
is with those who will not or cannot adjust to the platitudes of
conformity. He believes "in the unsmart, the unregulated and
the affectionate," in the fringe-dwellers of the early stories and
the beatniks of his later work. The conflict of attitudes which
lies at the heart of most of his writing, and in particular of
The Hangover gives rise to a technique bewildering to many.

Some of his critics have implied that he insists on mixing the unmixable; but to those who are not engaged in the futile quest for "the great New Zealand novel" or for an exemplification of academic theories on the art of the novel, he remains an unorthodox creator of new and unexpected fictions. According to D'Arcy Cresswell he was "the first wasp with a new and menacing buzz," and more than thirty years later he continues to excite and irritate with a newer and more menacing buzz.

CHAPTER 10

Epilogue

A S I have indicated earlier, the biography of a living writer presents difficulties which preclude anything in the nature of a definitive "Life." The preceding record has placed its main emphasis on what has been called "The Making of a New Zealander" and "The Making of a Writer" primarily because these aspects of Sargeson's early career have more than usual relevance to the problems of the literary artist in this country; they reveal facets of New Zealand life which should be taken into account before any evaluation is attempted. Nevertheless it should be apparent that the narrative contains some unavoidable gaps which, although unimportant in so far as the imaginative writing is concerned, would be more serious in a complete biography.

Throughout his life Sargeson has continued to be keenly aware of social, political and literary trends in New Zealand, but he has preferred to remain aloof and in comparative isolation. For more than thirty-five years he has lived alone in his Takapuna bach on the North Shore of Auckland Harbour. He has not felt it necessary to answer those critics who have asked: "Why don't you keep proper hours? Why is your garden so untidy when you spend so much time in it? Why don't you learn to behave yourself? Why do you associate with riff-raff who never have a penny to bless themselves with any more than you have? Why do you stay in New Zealand if you want to make your name?" Although still interested in law he has never sought to reenter the legal profession, but has adapted his life to the requirements of his creative work.

Owing to surgical tuberculosis he was not called up for war service and remained on an Invalidity Benefit until 1947, when through the aid of Sir Joseph Heenan (Under-Secretary of Internal Affairs) he was granted a small literary pension of three pounds a week. The pension was to be increased to four pounds after he had paid, at the rate of fifty-two pounds a year, for small extensions to his bach; but as this condition was not recorded in the Internal Affairs Department and Sir Joseph died in 1951, it was only through the help of John Reece Cole, chief librarian of the Turnbull Library, and himself a short-story writer, that the amount was augmented. On this he has managed to live, because under New Zealand publishing conditions his writing has never produced much in the way of financial reward.

Although he is among the very few New Zealand authors who have gained reputations overseas, Sargeson's influence has been confined to his own country, where his artistic dedication and integrity have been a source of encouragement to writers very different from himself; and many have had cause to remember his hospitality and kindness as well as his interest in their work. It can be argued, however, that his imaginative vision of reality and his individual style have been dangerous assets to an emerging literature. A writer of a younger generation, Dennis McEldowney, has observed:

I had never known adult books before there was Sargeson, and yet Sargeson was new. And I, too, believed that Sargeson's was the only possible kind of short story and his people the only true New Zealanders. This had not at all the emotional force of an *opinion:* it was something that *was.*[1]

Such a statement holds implications of possible stumbling-blocks, particularly for short-story writers who followed in the wake of Sargeson's endeavours, and it has been noticeable that a number of them did not always escape the tone and manner of their forerunner. Both a well-deserved tribute and a critical hesitancy are combined in the words of an anonymous wit, who asserted, "New Zealand literature has had two tragedies: the first was Katherine Mansfield, and the second is Frank Sargeson."

Notes and References

ABBREVIATIONS

C. S.   *Collected Stories, 1935-63.*
I. O.   *I for One.*
L.   *Landfall.*
M. P.   *Memoirs of a Peon.*
P. W.   *The Puritan and the Waif.*
R.   "Up onto the Roof and Down Again" (extracts published in *Landfall*).
R. (t).   Typescript of "Up onto the Roof and Down Again."
S. D.   *I Saw in My Dream.*
T.   *Tomorrow.*
W. A.   *Wrestling with the Angel.*
W. N.   "Writing a Novel" (typescript taken from tape).

PREFACE

1. "A Note from England," P. W., p. 19.
2. "The First Wasp," P. W., p. 1.
3. The manuscript of "Writing a Novel" has been lost. Quotations from the tape have been taken by permission of the New Zealand National Broadcasting Corporation and Frank Sargeson.

CHAPTER ONE

1. T., I, Oct. 9, 1935, p. 24.
2. "I Believe," P. W., p. 22.
3. S. D., p. 108.
4. S. D., p. 227.
5. R. (t).
6. C. S., p. 284.
7. C. S., pp. 284-285.
8. R. (t).
9. C. S., p. 287.

10. C. S., p. 284.
11. R. (t).
12. R. (t).
13. R. (t).
14. *New Zealand Listener,* June 10, 1949.
15. S. D., p. 98.
16. R., *Landfall,* IV, Dec., 1950, 286.
17. *Ibid.,* p. 288.
18. *Ibid.,* p. 285.
19. R., *Landfall,* V, Dec., 1951, 248.
20. R. (t).
21. *Ibid.*
22. *Ibid.*
23. *Ibid.*
24. R., *Landfall,* V, Dec., 1951, 247-250.
25. R. (t).

CHAPTER TWO

1. R. (t).
2. *Dominion,* Christchurch, Caxton Press, 1938.
3. *Collected Poems,* Christchurch, Pegasus Press, 1962.
4. T., II, Nov. 6, 1935.
5. "New Zealand: Answer to an Inquiry," *Horizon,* London, VIII, Sept., 1943, 156.
6. *The Bush,* Bernard O'Dowd, Melbourne, Thomas C. Lothian, 1912.
7. C. S., p. 67.
8. R. (t).
9. *Ibid.*
10. R., *Landfall,* V, June, 1951, 104-105.
11. R. (t).
12. "Beginnings," *Landfall,* XIX, June, 1965, 126n.
13. C. S., pp. 77-78.
14. "Beginnings", *Landfall,* XIX, June, 1965, 127.
15. *Ibid.,* p. 128.
16. *Landfall County,* ed. Charles Brasch, Christchurch, Caxton Press, 1962.

CHAPTER THREE

1. W. N.
2. "The Cultural Cringe," A. A. Phillips, *Meanjin,* IX, 1950, Summer.

3. T., III, Oct. 27, 1937, 822.
4. T., IV, Nov. 24, 1937, 55.
5. C. S., p. 257.
6. *Ibid.*, p. 78.
7. *Ibid.*, p. 138.
8. *Ibid.*, p. 116.
9. *Ibid.*, p. 150.
10. *Ibid.*, p. 151.
11. *New Zealand Monthly Review,* VI, June, 1965.
12. C. S., p. 22.
13. *Ibid.*, p. 24.
14. *Ibid.*, p. 65.
15. *Ibid.*, pp. 36-37.
16. L., XIX, June, 1965.
17. C. S., p. 153.
18. *Ibid.*, p. 256.
19. *Ibid.*, Prefatory Note, p. 20.
20. *Ibid.*, p. 55.
21. *Ibid.*, p. 106.
22. *Ibid.*, Introduction, p. 16n.
23. *Ibid.*, p. 100.
24. *Ibid.*, p. 75.
25. *Ibid.*, p. 27.
26. *Ibid.*, p. 97.
27. *Middlemarch,* Edinburgh and London, Blackwood, 1901, p. 104.
28. "Back to the Desert," P. W., p. 11.
29. C. S., p. 124.
30. *Ibid.*, p. 135.
31. *Ibid.*, p. 36.
32. *A Man and his Wife,* Christchurch, Caxton Press, 1940, p. 101.
33. C. S., p. 72.
34. *Ibid.*, p. 68.
35. *Ibid.*, p. 280.
36. *Ibid.*, p. 264.
37. *Ibid.*, pp. 272-273.
38. *Ibid.*, p. 43.
39. *Ibid.*, p. 46.
40. *Ibid.*, p. 110.
41. T., IV, Aug. 3, 1938, 626.
42. L., XIX, March, 1965, 5.
43. C. S., pp. 250-251.

44. "Beau," *Mate*, June, 1965, p. 19.
45. L., XIX, March, 1965, 4.
46. L., XVIII, June, 1964, 124.

CHAPTER FOUR

1. L., I, Sept., 1947, 220.
2. C. S., p. 176.
3. *Ibid.*, p. 166.
4. "Back to the Desert," P. W., p. 12.
5. C. S., p. 186.
6. *Ibid.*, p. 180.
7. *Ibid.*, pp. 157-158.
8. *Ibid.*, pp. 188-189.
9. *Ibid.*, pp. 203-204.
10. *TLS*, June 17, 1965.
11. C. S., p. 211.
12. *Ibid.*, pp. 238-239.
13. *Ibid.*, p. 239.
14. "On Tail-Chasing," *Collected Essays*, Sydney and London, Angus & Robertson, 1941, p. 99.
15. C. S., p. 182.
16. *Ibid.*, p. 234.
17. *Ibid.*, p. 33.

CHAPTER FIVE

1. "All Sorts of Stories," Neil Jillett, the *Age* (Melbourne), June, 1965.
2. W. N.
3. S. D., p. 99.
4. *The Pilgrim's Progress*, Oxford, Clarendon Press, 1960, p. 65.
5. "The First Wasp," P. W., p. 5.
6. *Ibid.*
7. S. D., p. 12.
8. *Ibid.*, p. 11.
9. *Ibid.*, p. 21.
10. *Ibid.*, p. 19.
11. *Ibid.*, pp. 17-18.
12. *Ibid.*, p. 25.
13. *Ibid.*, p. 79.
14. *Ibid.*, p. 11.
15. *Ibid.*, pp. 23-24.

16. *Ibid.,* p. 46.
17. *Ibid.,* pp. 31-32.
18. *Ibid.,* p. 65.
19. *Ibid.,* p. 69.
20. *Ibid.,* p. 80.
21. *Ibid.,* p. 93.
22. *Ibid.,* p. 98.
23. *Ibid.,* p. 127.
24. *Ibid.,* p. 170.
25. *Ibid.,* p. 169.
26. *Ibid.,* pp. 201-204.
27. *Ibid.,* p. 244.
28. "I Believe," P. W., p. 26.
29. S. D., p. 232.
30. *Ibid.,* p. 212.
31. *Ibid.,* pp. 219-220.
32. *Ibid.,* p. 158.
33. *Ibid.,* p. 277.
34. L., IV, June, 1950, 158.
35. *Ibid.,* p. 159.

CHAPTER SIX

1. L., X, Sept., 1956, 255.
2. I. O., p. 48.
3. *Ibid.,* p. 8.
4. *Ibid.,* p. 27.
5. *Ibid.,* p. 28.
6. *Ibid.,* p. 11.
7. *Ibid.,* p. 23.
8. *Ibid.,* p. 58.
9. *Ibid.,* p. 21.
10. *Loc. cit.*
11. *Ibid.,* p. 13.
12. *Ibid.,* p. 18.
13. *Ibid.,* p. 15.
14. *Ibid.,* p. 14.
15. *Ibid.,* p. 25.
16. *Ibid.,* p. 31.
17. *Ibid.,* p. 29.
18. *Ibid.,* pp. 43-44.
19. *Ibid.,* p. 56.

20. *Loc. cit.*
21. *Loc. cit.*

CHAPTER SEVEN

1. T., V, Dec. 7, 1938, 73-74.
2. *Ibid.*, p. 74.
3. T., V, Oct. 25, 1939, 816.
4. L., XVIII, March, 1964, 51.
5. *Ibid.*, p. 50.
6. "The Wide Open Cage," James Bertram, L., XIV, March, 1960, 81.
7. "Towards a New Zealand Drama," Erle Nelson, L., XVII, June, 1963, 122.
8. "A Time for Sowing," Allen Curnow, L., XV, March, 1961, 77.
9. *New Zealand Listener*, June 30, 1961.
10. W. A., p. 45.
11. *Ibid.*, p. 11.
12. *Ibid.*, p. 33.
13. "A Time for Sowing," Allen Curnow, L., XV, March, 1961, 79.
14. *Ibid.*, p. 78.
15. "Frank Sargeson's Play," W. S. Broughton, L., XV, Sept., 1961.
16. W. A., p. 93.
17. *Ibid.*, p. 92.
18. *Ibid.*, p. 120.
19. *Ibid.*, p. 119.
20. L., XVI, Sept., 1962, 297.
21. *Ibid.*, p. 298.

CHAPTER EIGHT

1. M. P., p. 6.
2. *Ibid.*, p. 178.
3. *Ibid.*, p. 239.
4. *Ibid.*, p. 7.
5. *Ibid.*, p. 31.
6. *Ibid.*, p. 80.
7. *Ibid.*, pp. 29-30.
8. *Ibid.*, p. 126.
9. *Ibid.*, p. 123.
10. *Ibid.*, pp. 171-172.
11. *Ibid.*, p. 200.
12. *Ibid.*, p. 50.

13. *Ibid.,* p. 140.
14. *Ibid.,* p. 44.
15. *Ibid.,* p. 134.
16. *Ibid.,* p. 281.

CHAPTER TEN

1. *New Zealand Monthly Review,* VI, June, 1965.

Selected Bibliography

A *Bibliography of Frank Sargeson's Imaginative Writing*, compiled by the editor, Bill Pearson, is appended to *Collected Stories, 1935-63*, Auckland, Blackwood and Janet Paul, in conjunction with MacGibbon & Kee (London), 1964. Includes published volumes, imaginative writing in periodicals and a detailed account of previous appearances of Sargeson's Short Stories. A Bibliography of published volumes (to 1950) may be found in *The Puritan and the Waif* (out of print), edited by Helen Shaw and issued in an edition of 50 cyclostyled copies, Auckland, H. L. Hofmann, 1954.

PRIMARY SOURCES

Conversation with my Uncle and Other Sketches, Auckland, Unicorn Press, 1936.

A Man and his Wife, Christchurch, Caxton Press, 1940. Cheap Edition, 1941. New Edition, revised, Wellington, Progressive Publishing Society, 1944. Cheap printing, 1944.

That Summer and Other Stories, London, John Lehmann, 1946. A French translation by Jeanne Fournier-Pargoire, *Cet été-là*, Paris, Editions du Bateau-Ivre, 1946.

When the Wind Blows, Christchurch, Caxton Press, 1945. (The first section of *I Saw in My Dream*.) Cheap edition, 1948.

Speaking for Ourselves (ed. Frank Sargeson), Christchurch, Caxton Press and Reed & Harris (Melbourne). A collection of stories by Australian and New Zealand writers.

I Saw in My Dream, London, John Lehmann, 1949.

I for One, Christchurch, Caxton Press, 1954 (but published in 1956).

Collected Stories, 1935-63, with an Introduction by Bill Pearson, Auckland, Blackwood and Janet Paul, in conjunction with MacGibbon & Kee (London), 1964.

Wrestling with the Angel, Two Plays: A Time for Sowing and The Cradle & The Egg, Christchurch, Caxton Press, 1964.

Memoirs of a Peon, London, MacGibbon & Kee (London), 1965.

The Hangover, London, MacGibbon & Kee (London), 1967.

Note: Since the publication in 1964 of Pearson's *Bibliography, etc.*, the following imaginative writings have appeared in periodicals:

"Just Trespassing, Thanks," *Landfall*, June 1964.

"City and Suburban," *Landfall*, March 1965.

"Beau," Auckland, *Mate*, June 1965.

"Beginnings," *Landfall*, June 1965.

"Summer Days (from Work in Progress)," Auckland, *Mate*, August 1966.

"Charity Begins at Home," Christchurch, *Landfall*, September 1966.

"An Imaginary Conversation, William Yate and Samuel Butler," Christchurch, *Landfall*, December 1966.

"A Final Cure," *Landfall*, June 1967.

"Breakfast with the Reverend" (from Work in Progress), *New Zealand Monthly Review*, August, 1967.

"Conversation in a Train," *Landfall*, December 1967.

Also of interest, not mentioned by Pearson is "Old Goat, Young Lamb," Melbourne, *Southern Stories, Poems and Paintings*, Dolphin Publications (no date), an extract from *When the Wind Blows*.

"Writing a Novel," the unpublished script of two radio talks by Frank Sargeson, taken from tape by permission of the New Zealand Broadcasting Corporation.

SECONDARY SOURCES

BRASCH, CHARLES (ed.). "The Moral Climate of Sargeson's Stories," *Landfall Country*, Christchurch, Caxton Press, 1962. Reprinted from *Landfall*, March 1955. Originally appeared in *The Puritan and the Waif*.

CHAPMAN, ROBERT. "Fiction and the Social Pattern," *Landfall*, Christchurch, Caxton Press, March 1953.

HORSMAN, E. A. "The Art of Frank Sargeson," *Landfall*, Christchurch, Caxton Press, June 1965.

McCORMICK, E. H. In *New Zealand Literature, A Survey*, London, Oxford University Press, 1959.

PEARSON, BILL. Introduction to *Collected Stories, 1935-63*, Frank Sargeson, Auckland, Blackwood and Janet Paul, 1964.

PLOMER, WILLIAM. "Some Books from New Zealand," *Penguin New Writing*, No. 17, London, Allen Lane, 1943.

RHODES, H. WINSTON. "The Stories of Frank Sargeson," *New Zealand Libraries*, Wellington, N. Z. Library Association, September 1947.

SHAW, HELEN (ed.). *The Puritan and the Waif, A Symposium of Critical Essays on the Work of Frank Sargeson*, Auckland, H. L. Hofmann, 1954, issued in an edition of 50 cyclostyled copies, second printing of 50 copies, 1955. Essays by D'Arcy Cresswell, James K. Baxter, Walter Allen, E. P. Dawson, H. Winston Rhodes, Erik Schwimmer, Helen Shaw, and Dan Davin.

STEVENS, JOAN. In *The New Zealand Novel 1860-1960*, Wellington-Auckland, A. H. & A. W. Reed, 1961.

Index